Keeping Secrets

Mary E. Lyons

· · · · · · ·

Keeping Secrets

THE GIRLHOOD
DIARIES OF SEVEN
WOMEN WRITERS

HENRY HOLT
AND COMPANY
New York

Henry Holt and Company, Inc.
Publishers since 1866
115 West 18th Street
New York, New York 10011

Henry Holt is a registered
trademark of Henry Holt and Company, Inc.

Published in Canada by Fitzhenry & Whiteside Ltd.,
195 Allstate Parkway, Markham, Ontario L3R 4T8.

Library of Congress Cataloging-in-Publication Data
Lyons, Mary (Mary E.)
    Keeping secrets: the girlhood diaries of seven women writers/
by Mary E. Lyons.
        p.   cm.
Includes bibliographical references.
1. American diaries—Women authors—History and criticism—
Juvenile literature. 2. Girls—United States—Diaries—History
and criticism—Juvenile literature. 3. Women authors, American—
19th century—Biography—Juvenile literature.   [1. Authors, American.
2. Women—Biography. 3. Diaries.]   I. Title.
PS409.L96   1995   818'.303099287—dc20   94-36139

ISBN 0-8050-3065-4

First Edition—1995

Designed by Victoria Hartman

Printed in the United States of America
on acid-free paper. ∞

10 9 8 7 6 5 4 3 2 1

For T. L., age fifteen

One girl.
One girl reads this and takes fire!
Her life is changed. She becomes a power—
a mover of others—
I write for her.
                    —*Charlotte Perkins Gilman's diary*
                    December 26, 1932

Contents

❧

Acknowledgments

❧

$\mathscr{I}$ am grateful to the following for their help:

Marc Aronson suggested a book on diaries; Art Collier shared his insights on *The Awakening,* and his enthusiasm for Louisa May Alcott propelled me through that chapter; Wendy Thomas at the Schlesinger Library, Radcliffe College, went beyond the call of duty to make Charlotte Perkins Gilman's diaries available; Denise Knight generously sent portions of the manuscript of her book, *The Diaries of Charlotte Perkins Gilman;* Ann Lane kindly directed me to Denise Knight. Thanks to Paul Collinge for everything, for always.

Keeping Secrets

Dear Diary

The writing of *Keeping Secrets* has been a journey back to my own growing up. Before starting the trip, I decided to keep a diary for company along the way. A diarist long ago at fifteen, I wanted to remember how it felt to put thoughts on paper instead of locking them in my head. The idea made me uncomfortable at first, like being trapped in an elevator or flying through a thunderstorm. What dangerous emotions might drift to the surface if I explored the hidden parts of my grown-up self?

Soon after my pencil touched paper, unexpected feelings did appear, but in the form of a poem. I've discovered the secret pleasure of jumping into a pile of verbs and adjectives, then tossing them around until they look just right. A closet poet has been there all along, waiting to be released by my old friend, the diary.

My "cher ami" has also helped me better understand the seven women writers in *Keeping Secrets*. Sometimes I see them gathered in one room, as close as sisters. Corsets loosened, they sprawl over Victorian sofas and feast on old-fashioned gingerbread, a treat that many of them baked as girls. There is much laughing and talking as they reveal the special secrets that only young women can share. Still, some things are too private to tell anyone—except a diary.

As young adults, all of these writers kept a personal journal. The words they wrote in solitude in the nineteenth century let us eavesdrop on their inner thoughts today. Three of them wrote about secrets of the heart: Charlotte Forten, a free black abolitionist, was deeply attached to a man she could not marry. A teacher, Sarah Jane Foster kept a diary that knew about her forbidden sweetheart long before she did. And romance occasionally flickers in Kate Chopin's diary, though some of her secrets were so shocking that she had to create other women to tell them for her.

Keeping secrets gave the diarists a sense of power over family members—parents, brothers and sisters, husbands. But a secret only imparts power when someone else knows that it exists. Four of the women found ways to inform snoops that tempting secrets were hidden in their diaries. Charlotte Perkins Gilman disguised some of her private thoughts in shorthand. Alice Dunbar-Nelson wrote a fictionalized diary that dropped clues about her miserable marriage to poet Paul Laurence Dunbar. Ida B. Wells, anti-lynching crusader, may have removed the only page in her diary that knew the *real* reason why she quit school at sixteen.

Louisa May Alcott, author of *Little Women,* was the most direct of all. She left strict instructions to keep spies from peeking at her secret self: "These journals are kept only for my own reference," she insisted. "I particularly desire that if I die before I destroy them that they may *all* be *burned* unseen or copied by any one."

Despite the diarists' fears of discovery, their journals still survive—many thousands of pages that span almost one hundred years, from 1843 to 1931. Reading the diaries has reminded me that women's interests are timeless. Although we are on the eve of the twenty-first century, we can still identify with Kate Chopin's silent contempt for conformity in 1867 or Ida Wells's helpless frustration over racism in 1885. Some of us might share Sarah Foster's troubles with bullying bosses or Alice Dunbar-Nelson's worries about money.

Women's concerns are universal, too. Like many women throughout the world today, some of the diarists in *Keeping Secrets* lacked an education that would have given them confidence and earning power. Few received the encouragement they needed to find a fulfilling career. Domestic duties overwhelmed most: "In addition to other cares, a perfect WEIGHT of sewing presses upon me," wrote nineteen-year-old Charlotte Forten in 1857.

The diaries have also helped me remember the rough spots on the road to growing up. "Dear Diary," wrote Charlotte Perkins when she was fifteen years old. "Feeling tired, cross, lazy, stupid, mean, hungry, foolish, dispirited, disgusted, everything disagreeable." Charlotte scribbled these words in 1876, yet they are remarkably similar to ones I wrote in my diary at fifteen: "It's all so stupid, & I'm all so bewildered I don't know what to do. I'm going to have to face this whole thing alone & I sure hope I can get through it!"

The crisis—my first dance—was one that Charlotte never had to meet. She had other problems, though: an absent father, "homely" boys who wanted to kiss her, a demanding mother, not enough clothes to wear. Charlotte and I were born in different centuries, but we both fled to our diaries for comfort when no one else cared.

No matter the century, young women will always get mad

at their parents, argue with brothers and sisters, and fall in and out of love. For instance, only my diary knew how insanely boy-crazy I was at fifteen. I even made a list on the last page of the boys I had kissed. Three years later I scratched out several names (*gross* names, like Stanley and Duke) and wrote, "How could I!!!" Then I carefully recorded the date to prove how much older and wiser I had become.

I was a bit relieved to find out that fifteen-year-old Charlotte Perkins was wild about boys too. She fell madly in love with a "dear, darling, lovely, handsome, tall, graceful, splendid, glorious, excruciating, gorgeous" actor she never met. Nor was I the only person to go back and censor earlier diary entries. Fifty years after keeping their girlhood diaries, Charlotte Perkins Gilman and Louisa May Alcott reread the entries and inserted comments to explain their adolescent behavior.

At fifteen, I often wanted to scream with impatience, excitement, or frustration. My younger self used capital letters, underlining, and lots of exclamation points. These gave me a way to yell at the world without anyone hearing me.

Often frustrated by their female roles, the diarists in *Keeping Secrets* sometimes felt like yelling too. At the beginning of the 1800s, the typical American family lived and worked side by side on a farm. Some of the labor—weaving, milking, carrying water—was shared by men and women. But many of the jobs were divided by sex: men made the cradles that women rocked, butchered the meat that women cooked, grew the flax that women spun into linen and sewed into clothes.

As America became industrialized, meatpacking industries, furniture factories, and textile mills took over tasks formerly completed by men. Industrialization changed the nature of women's chores too, but not the number. Manufactured cloth meant no more long hours at the spinning wheel. But it also meant more sets of clothing for each family member, which resulted in more sewing and laundry.

While women remained at home doing the same preindustrial jobs, middle-class husbands went to work every day in a factory, business, or profession. There was no better proof of a man's success than a wife and daughter who stayed behind to do the washing, cleaning, and child care. Even now, many people think of these domestic jobs as "women's work," though most women are employed outside the home.

Nineteenth-century ministers preached sermons about the sacred domestic duties of women. Magazines like *Godey's Ladies Book* broadcast the message that "good women" were managers *and* ornaments of the home. And mothers expected daughters to share these roles with them. So every aspect of a middle-class girl's life, from her clothes to her education, kept her at home, "working like nature, in secret."

Simply taking a walk must have been difficult for fifteen-year-old Kate Chopin, who wears a hooped skirt in her 1865 photograph. A cage of steel wire hangs from her waist. Over the cage are layers of fabric weighing as much as thirty pounds. The hooped skirt hides the lower part of Kate's body, but it also emphasizes her hips. According to nineteenth-century standards of beauty, exaggeration of the female form made girls more sexually attractive.

The 1898 photograph of Alice Dunbar-Nelson suggests that she agreed to the tortures of a corset. To make her waist look smaller and her breasts appear larger, Alice hooked the corset around her waist. Then she sucked in her breath while her mother pulled the laces tight. Because the bone stays poked into her flesh, the corset made breathing difficult and bending over impossible. With brand names like *Armorside* ("Never Breaks Down on the Sides"), it is no surprise that corsets could break girls' ribs or cause their lungs to collapse. The only time Charlotte Perkins wore one, she almost fainted.

When I was in high school, I often dumped a wretched mood on my diary: "Crummy day! Everything went wrong," I wrote at the beginning of my tenth-grade year. "Had homework in every subject! Damn school! WISH IT WAS SUMMER!" But daughters in middle-class nineteenth-century homes wished they *could* go to school. Books and learning were much more interesting than cleaning house or sewing ties for a brother to wear to *his* school, as Charlotte Perkins did.

Charlotte's mother tutored her at home when she was a little girl, and Charlotte Forten received private instruction until she was fifteen. Such home schooling was typical, since there were no public high schools or colleges for women when they were growing up. None of the writers in *Keeping Secrets* obtained a four-year college degree. To pursue a higher education, they had to join an informal study group, enroll in random classes when money and time allowed, or read on their own (all of them loved *Jane Eyre,* a novel that begins with girlhood rebellion).

After the Civil War, human rights activists established girls' high schools and colleges. Around the turn of the century, they insisted on more comfortable clothing for women. Yet today's young women remain restricted in their education and physical movement. They have to argue for equal sports programs in schools and admission to tax-supported, all-male colleges. They struggle for the freedom to move through the world without fear of being raped, then blamed for it. Kate Chopin's comment in her 1869 diary—"I wonder what people thought of me—a young woman strolling about alone"—sounds sadly up-to-date for a girl out by herself.

I wrote in my girlhood diary for only nine months. Still, it helped me make some important changes. At first, I worried myself sick over grades and talked so much in class that a frustrated teacher once yelled at me. By the time I abandoned the diary, I had decided to be "a little bit more carefree" about "good marks" (a party girl was in the making). And I am sure my teachers were relieved that I finally gained some control over my mouth.

Most of the writers in *Keeping Secrets* kept diaries for years. Diary writing allowed each to escape the pressures of being a girl so that another self could start to grow. In the privacy of their diaries they could express anger, sexual desire, pride, despair. They could experiment with forbidden roles as adventurer, mistress, professor, or politician. Eventually they transformed these secret voices into public voices. And through their poetry, novels, articles, autobiographies, and published diaries, we can still hear them speak.

· · · · ·

"The Children's Friend"

✿

$\mathscr{L}$ouisa May Alcott wanted to be a good girl more than anything else in the world. Even as a two-year-old, though, her strong will was a powerful presence in the Alcott household in Boston, Massachusetts. She threw food at the supper table, slapped her older sister, Anna, and defied her father with a passion that exhausted him. "Her *force*," Bronson Alcott wrote wearily in his own diary, "makes me retreat sometimes from an encounter."

Bronson and Louisa were like crossed sticks throughout her childhood. She tried to behave, but he thought she was "obstinate" and often put her to bed "without the usual story or parting caress." When punishment did not dissolve her stubborn streak, he devised moral lessons to teach self-control. "Should little girls take things that do not belong to them—things to eat or drink?" he asked his daughters one day in the dining room. "No," each answered like a baby parrot. Then he placed an apple within easy reach and left them to fight temptation alone.

When he returned, he saw an apple core resting beside Louisa's plate at the table. "Why did you take it before father said you might have it?" Bronson asked, setting her on his knee. She wiggled like a worm, but her smile was as sweet as sorghum. "I wanted it," she replied.

In 1868, thirty-five-year-old Louisa May Alcott finally found a way to be an obedient daughter. She created an entire family of good girls in *Little Women: Meg, Jo, Beth and Amy. The Story of Their Lives. A Girl's Book.* The four daughters in *Little Women* are the fictional counterparts of the Alcott sisters: Anna, Louisa, Lizzie, and May. Louisa's mother, Abba, appears as the saintly Marmee, and she transformed Bronson into Papa, the holy father of the March family.

Little Women was an instant success. The first two thousand copies sold quickly, and millions more have since been printed around the world. For over one hundred and thirty years, the trials and triumphs of the March family have delighted young readers. Why is their story such a timeless classic?

Little Women wrapped its readers in the warm wool of familiarity. Nineteenth-century girls enjoyed the feminine finery—pearl pins, silk gloves, curling irons—that beribboned the plot. And girls who spent most of their time at home felt reassured when the March sisters sewed sheets, fried cakes, mended clothes, and had teatime, just as they did. Like many other novels of the day, *Little Women* reinforced a conventional belief in marriage, motherhood, and home as a girl's proper destiny.

But most of that wholesome literature was written in a melodramatic style that contrasts with *Little Women*'s lively humor. "I hate affected, niminy-piminy chits!" Jo March declares in nineteenth-century slang. Jo, like her counterpart, Louisa, is a tomboy with a "quick temper, sharp tongue, and restless spirit." Although she is "always getting into scrapes," she struggles to become the perfect girl (a little woman). Readers love her, not when she succeeds, but because she usually fails.

Some aspects of *Little Women* are puzzling, however. At first, the book seems to be a moral tale for girls: "We can make little sacrifices," Meg preaches to her sisters on the first page of the book. Yet underneath its do-good surface is a perverse layer of rebellion.

Louisa May Alcott claimed she never wanted to marry. "I'd rather be a free spinster and paddle my own canoe," she told her diary. Then why did she lock her fictional self into a marriage? Why did she wed Jo to a frumpy older man instead of the boyish, handsome Laurie? And if she admired her "brave" and "serene" father, why did she reduce his character in the book to a mere shadow? These riddles add spice to the homey pot-roast flavor of *Little Women.* They show how the author used her pen to create a subtle escape from reality.

Louisa learned how to be a good girl so well that she had no life of her own after she grew up. Caught in a snood of self-sacrifice as nursemaid, housekeeper, or breadwinner, she always put the needs of her family first. The real Louisa lived behind the mask of a dutiful daughter. But sometimes in her diary, then as the mysterious author "A. M. Barnard," and finally in *Little Women,* she dropped this domestic disguise. In these texts Louisa May Alcott resisted her good girl role and played tricks on her readers and even herself.

Childhood

· *1832–1843* ·

$\mathcal{I}$t is no wonder that Louisa felt tied down to her mother and father. Her identity as the daughter of Abba and Bronson Alcott was sealed from the day she was born. A "fine, healthful" baby, she arrived in 1832 on her father's birthday, November 29. Abba's family name, May, became the infant girl's middle name. How could little Louy ever feel independent when she had to share her name with her mother and every birthday with her father?

Bronson Alcott recorded his daughter's birth in his diary, but he could have been writing about the arrival of new puppies instead of a baby girl. "This is a most interesting event," he coolly noted. The words expose a dreamy detachment from his feelings, fatherhood, and the practical demands of life.

Louisa's father was part of a movement known as Transcendentalism. In the 1820s a group of former students from Harvard Divinity School rejected the idea of organized religion, including the popular Unitarianism. Unitarians were too worldly, claimed Transcendentalists like Ralph Waldo Emerson and Henry David Thoreau. The route to salvation did not include churches or ministers, they said. Only appreciation of nature, rejection of material pleasures, and self-reflection could bring enlightenment.

Shy, gangly, thin-haired Bronson was attracted to this philosophy of solitude. He especially liked the idea of self-discovery through keeping a diary. He could record every event, then dissect it for its spiritual lesson. Beginning with a goose-quill pen at the age of twelve, he wrote in a diary almost every day for the rest of his life. By the age of eighty-eight, he had filled thirty thousand pages with five million words.

The diaries were not just a record of Bronson Alcott's life. They *were* his life. Unable to express deep emotion, he sometimes substituted them for himself. When he was courting Abba, for example, he gave her sixty diary pages to read rather than speak his feelings aloud. "We know we *love her*— we *almost* believe that she loves us," he wrote, using the royal "we." "Let us enjoy the pleasing idea."

Diaries were so important to him that every member of his family kept one, whether they wanted to or not. Once Louisa was "unfaithful" to her diary, and Bronson made her eat supper alone. A journal of conscience, this was hardly the place for a child to store a secret: "Father asked us all what faults we watted [wanted] to get rid of," his ten-year-old daughter wrote early in 1843. "I said impatience."

To check for moral growth, both Bronson and Abba peeked at Louisa's girlhood diaries. Sometimes her mother even slipped a note between the pages. "DEAR LOUY," she instructed the daughter who had her own dark hair and blue eyes, "remember, dear girl, that a diary should be an epitome of your life. May it be a record of pure thought and good actions, then you will indeed be the precious child of your loving mother."

Abba wanted Louisa to be an ideal daughter, just as she idealized her own mother, who "adored her husband and children" and "went about doing good." With no formal education or profession of her own, Abba also made it her job to be a good wife. From the beginning of the Alcotts' courtship, she felt responsible for Bronson's finances. "He is poor," she worried in a letter to her brother. "I do think the ladies ought to remunerate him generously. . . . I feel anxious for his means."

Her outlook fit perfectly with the Transcendental view of the sexes: men were creatures of intellect and justice, women were sympathetic and full of compassion. But caring for her "good, mild, vague, and somewhat absurd" husband eventually stole all of Abba's strength, a burden she bequeathed to Louisa. And Louisa, raised to be a good little Transcendentalist, shouldered the load.

Meanwhile, Bronson allowed himself the luxury of a simple philosophy. "I set out from the ground of Spirit," he wrote in his diary. "This *is*. All else is its manifestation." His deeply spiritual nature inspired everyone who knew him, including his wife and children. Unfortunately for his family, though, "all else" included earning a living.

At first he supported the family by teaching school in Boston, but parents fired him when he substituted moral lessons for geography and arithmetic. Discouraged, he decided to live near Emerson and Thoreau, his Transcendental companions (both men later became Louisa's tutors). He moved his family to Concord, Massachusetts, where he earned money by chopping wood for a dollar a day. Then Bronson concluded that working for a wage was morally wrong—he should only accept money, not earn it. So he decided to give spiritual lectures and ask for donations.

Louisa often felt afraid and ashamed when she was growing up. Where would the money come from if her father refused to work? "I don't see who is to clothe and feed us all," the frightened girl once wrote, "when we are so poor now." How anxious she must have been, watching Bronson sit under a tree as he waited for passersby to stop, listen, and give—knowing there would be only apples and rice for dinner that night.

And the more she worried, the more she misbehaved. One day she spoke "unkindly" to her younger sisters and was "disobedient to mother and father." On the next she was "gentle" with her sisters and "obedient and kind to Father and Mother." Louisa's unpredictable behavior was a barometer of the family's unstable life. They frequently lived on the charity of friends and relatives, relocating to another town or house almost every year of her childhood.

Fruitlands
• 1843–1845 •

Despite the poverty, there were many loving, cheerful times in the Alcott family. They were poor, but fun was free. Bronson enjoyed being a teacher to his four daughters. He let them build "houses and bridges" in the study with his diaries and dictionaries and lay on the floor while they traced letters in the air with his spindly legs.

The girls put on plays in the barn with an ever-changing cast of dolls and cats. Like the colorful characters she would later create, Louisa's babies were "fed, educated, punished, rewarded, nursed, and even hung and buried." One Concord playmate remembered that Louisa's theatrics made his "sides ache with laughter."

Most of these carefree moments disappeared in 1843 when Bronson helped start "Fruitlands," a Transcendentalist farming community. The experiment was a bitter failure that almost destroyed the Alcotts' marriage. The rules of the community were clear: No animals could be used to provide labor, meat, or dairy products. No leather could be worn, only tunics of brown linen. Meals occasionally consisted of "cakes" made of maple sugar, dried peas, and grains, but most were a simple course of bread, fruit, and water. For some reason even salt was forbidden.

Abba was the only woman in the community of seven men. She prepared all the food, starting with breakfast at five A.M. and ending with a late afternoon supper. The severe schedule and spartan diet made her wonder in her diary if she would go mad.

Young Louisa absorbed her mother's misery. Thirty years later she avenged Abba in a parody of the Fruitlands fiasco called *Transcendental Wild Oats*. In this brief satire, a newcomer asks if there are any beasts of burden at Fruitlands. The character of Sister Hope (Abba) answers, "Only one woman!"

Shortly before moving to Fruitlands, Bronson wrote a note to Louisa about her "anger, discontent, impatience, evil appetites, greedy wants, complainings, ill-speakings, vileness, heedlessness, and rude behavior." No wonder she used language in her Fruitlands diary that would please her parents! "I was cross to-day, and I cried when I went to bed," she confessed to her diary-mother-father. "I made good resolutions, and felt better in my heart. If only I *kept* all I make, I should be the best girl in the world. But I don't, and so am very bad."

Still, angry feelings sometimes erupted in the landscape of penitent words. "I hate her," Louisa wrote of her music teacher, "she is so fussy." And when Abba wanted to divorce Bronson because she was "so tired," Louisa fled to her diary with the awful news. "Anna and I cried in bed," she confided, "and I prayed God to keep us all together."

An underground diary where Louisa recorded fantasies helped her cope with her parents' problems. "I wrote in my Imagination Book and enjoyed it very much," she told her diary. "Life is pleasanter than it used to be and I don't care about dying any more." Louisa had discovered how to make sweet illusion replace hard reality.

The dark days at Fruitlands finally ended when the community fell apart in 1845. By then, Louisa was twelve years old, an age when a girl craves privacy, especially from her family. But her diary was still a bow to her father's beliefs. She had to figure out a way to make diary writing private and personal. Only then could it give her the power she needed to become herself.

Heart-Journal
• *1846–1847* •

*L*ouisa was absolutely certain she needed a space of her own. "I have been thinking about my little room which I suppose I never shall have," she pouted in a note to her mother when she was twelve. "I should want to be there about all the time and I should go there and sing and think." And be alone! Louisa did not write the words, but it is easy to sense her longing for a retreat.

A year later, in 1846, her wish came true when the Alcotts moved into a house near Emerson's home in Concord. "I have at last got the little room I have wanted so long," the thirteen-year-old exulted in her diary, "and am very happy about it. It does me good to be alone, and Mother has made it very pretty and neat for me." The room opened onto a garden that led to the woods—an idyllic place for a young girl to grow into womanhood.

Immediately she cuddled up with her diary and told it a secret. "I have made a plan for my life, as I am in my teens, and no more a child," she wrote in the only surviving entry of her 1846 diary. "I have not told any one about my plan; but I'm going to *be* good."

Despite the vow, though, her behavior worsened, and Bronson grew so exasperated that he mentioned her only once in his diary that year. "I had a Possessed One sitting by my side all winter," he brooded, a daughter whose "will was bound in chains" by devils. Why was fourteen-year-old Louisa so hardheaded? Perhaps her rebellion gave voice to the secret that no one could say aloud: the real "possessed one" in the family was Bronson, who hid his neglect behind a sincere but self-centered piety.

Louisa depended on her diary to survive these confusing years. When she turned fifteen, she began what she later called her "romantic period." Too restless to sleep, she roamed around the yard in the moonlight when everyone else was in bed. She wrote great lumps of maudlin verse and kept a "heart-journal."

Although she later destroyed the 1847 diary, it probably recorded a crush on her teacher, "Mr. Emerson." Years later, Louisa said she left anonymous bouquets on the poet's door-step and shyly sang a serenade under his window. When Emerson lent her a book about a young girl who writes worshipful letters to an older man, Louisa was inspired to do the same. With long legs dangling from the bough of a cherry tree, the lovesick young woman wrote notes to the man she later called the "god" of her "idolatry."

We can only imagine her words of adulation, for she never sent the letters. Like the diaries from 1846 and 1847, she later burned them. Guarding her girlhood secrets must have given the grown-up Louisa some sense of control over her life. And though we long to read these diaries and letters now, their destruction proves one thing: Young Louisa had discovered the magic of hiding secret thoughts inside written words.

Work
• 1848–1861 •

When the family moved to Boston in 1848, Louisa lost her cherished sanctuary. Maybe this is why she chose not to keep a diary during 1848 and 1849. We know none of her secrets as a sixteen- and seventeen-year-old, only that when she resumed her diary a year later, in 1850, she remembered "fine free times alone" and "silly thoughts."

The 1850 journal marked the start of her "working days," when she began to sculpt the mask of obligation she wore for the rest of her life. These times were difficult for the family. They all had smallpox that summer. While Bronson gave lectures in his "clear musical voice," the Alcott women patched together an income: Anna by teaching, Louisa as a maid and governess, Abba as a paid visitor to the poor. Lizzie, then fifteen, and May, ten, were too young to work.

Louisa hated her various odd jobs. They deepened her resolve to save the family from poverty. "My dream is to have a lovely, quiet home for her [mother], with no debt or troubles to burden her," she fantasized in her diary. "[Anna] must have a good time in a nice little home of her own some day, as we often plan." Strangely, she left her father out of the rosy vision. Maybe she blamed him for the veil of duty she had to don in her late teen years. Like Jo March, she thought she had to become "the man of the family."

Where did Louisa's sense of duty come from? After a childhood of scrupulous faultfinding, the seventeen-year-old young woman seemed encased, like amber, in guilt. "In the quiet I see my faults," she wrote, "and try to mend them; but, deary me, I don't get on at all." If ever she forgot her shortcomings, Bronson was there to remind her. "In looking over our journals, Father says, 'Anna's is about other people, Louisa's about herself,' " she remarked in the diary in May 1850.

Then she discovered a way to fulfill her duty and escape from it too, just as she had done in her diaries. In 1851, nineteen-year-old Louisa wrote her first published short story, "The Masked Marriage." When she sold it for ten dollars, she proudly noted the amount in the back of her book. But like the anonymous stories she later produced, "The Masked Marriage" brought her more than money. It was the beginning of what one biographer has called an "Alternative Alcott."

"The Masked Marriage" features a young "Lady Viola," who tricks her father at a masked ball so she can marry the man she loves. At first, Louisa's choice of subject matter seems odd. Why would she want to write about marriage?

She pitied her mother, whose life as Mrs. Alcott was "so full of wandering and all sorts of worry." Years later, middle-aged Louisa noted that she knew little about marriage "except observing that very few were happy ones."

Besides, the young woman with a waterfall of wavy brown hair showed little interest in the opposite sex. All elbows and knees, she felt clumsy around boys. Perhaps she believed the insensitive note that Abba gave her on her fifteenth birthday: "Your temperament is a peculiar one," wrote her mother, "and there are few or none that can intelligently help you."

With advice like this, she would have found it difficult to relax with men. Once, when a man "gushed" over her on the train, her sisters "laughed and had great fun over Jo's [Louisa's] lover." "My adorers are all queer [odd]," Louisa ruefully told her diary.

Still, the idea of romance and marriage tempted her, though she could not imagine it as a happy state. Through writing, she transformed herself into "lovely Viola radiant with joy and beauty." She drifted though "stately halls" and "orange groves sleeping in the moonlight." Louisa's story let her briefly redesign her humdrum life.

And it let her use trickery on a fictional father. Although she might not have admitted it to herself, some embers of resentment must have smoldered in her mind. Now in her twenties, her duties increased as she took over Bronson's role. She used all of her earnings to care for the family, buying gowns for her sisters while she wore hand-me-downs from cousins and friends. "I seem to be the only breadwinner right now," she wrote in 1858.

Bronson forced her to bear the burdens of a man, yet she had none of a man's freedom. During the 1850s she rarely mentioned him in her diary, remarking only once a year on his progress as a wage earner: "Father wrote and talked when he could," she wrote in 1852—"Father doing as well as a philosopher can in a money-loving world," she commented in 1854. And she was of little interest to him—he referred to her in his diary only twice between 1850 and 1860.

Meanwhile, her writing career rolled along as smoothly as a hoop. She lavished motherly attention on her first published book, a collection of children's fables that she called her "first-born." In a faltering attempt to separate from her parents, twenty-three-year-old Louisa moved to Boston. There she wrote stories in a private "sky-parlor"—an attic in a boardinghouse. She loved the "freedom and independence" of being on her own. But in the spring of 1856 she returned to Concord to care for her dying younger sister, Lizzie. (Louisa later transformed Lizzie into the character of Beth in *Little Women*.)

Bronson seemed unable to stay at home during Lizzie's sad decline. "Father decides to go back to Concord," Louisa wrote in her diary; "he is never happy far from Emerson." "Father goes on a trip West taking Grandma with him," she noted in 1857. He returned in time to hold Lizzie in his arms as she died, but again, the Alcott women had carried on without his help.

The Civil War
• 1861–1863 •

Being female chafed twenty-nine-year-old Louisa like one of Jo March's starched collars. "I long to be a man," she protested to her diary when the Civil War started in 1861, "but as I can't fight, I will content myself with working for those who can." She did not really want to be a man—she simply wanted to do the things men could do. As curious as any young soldier about war, she turned again to writing to create alternate adventures for herself.

Starting that year, she wrote "thrillers" under a pseudonym that sounds like a man's name: A. M. Barnard. Like the title of her first published story, these titles vibrate with intrigue and deception: "Whisper in the Dark," "A Pair of Eyes: Modern Magic," "Pauline's Passion and Punishment." A pen name let her delve anonymously into the dark themes of suicide, mind control, illegal drugs, and even incest— topics not thought suitable for women writers. With guilty relief, she shared the pleasures of secret writing with her diary: "I enjoy romancing to suit myself," she admitted, "and though my tales are silly, they are not bad; and my sinners always have a good spot somewhere."

Midway through the bloody war, Louisa's tales grew even more sensational. In 1863 she decided she was tired of knitting and sewing for Union soldiers. "Help needed and I love nursing," she proclaimed in her diary, "and [I] *must* let out my pent-up energy in some new way." Hungry for fresh experiences, the thirty-year-old woman felt like a son tramping off to war when she traveled to a Union hospital in Washington, D.C.

She longed to follow the fighting, but settled instead for nursing the "helpless boys" who lay wounded in the hospital. Louisa's diary became her "idea box." Here she recorded the gory details that later appeared in her first best-selling book, *Hospital Sketches*. In only two weeks, though, the "bad air, food, water, work & watching" left her exhausted and sick with pneumonia. In a rare show of fatherliness, Bronson arrived to take his daughter home to Concord, where she recovered after three weeks of fever and delirium.

Although she almost lost her life, the illness produced a shocking store of details to recycle into thrillers. Now Louisa filled her "idea box" with images remembered from her feverish dreams: weird visions of heaven, devils, witches burned at the stake, and a "Spanish spouse" who threatened her "dreadfully all night long."

When she recovered, she continued to write moral tales for children while producing a string of subversive stories that signified her dual life: "A Double Tragedy," "Enigmas," "A Marble Woman: or the Mysterious Model." With them she plunged more deeply into forbidden territory, including opium addiction and a favorite theme that recalled her infatuation with Emerson: the pairing of an older man with a child bride.

Behind a Mask
• 1866–1868 •

After the war ended, Louisa made a "long desired dream" come true—she began a year of travel through Europe. Working as a paid companion, she accompanied a young invalid named Anna Weld. Anna turned out to be a "fidgety" and demanding patient, and much of the trip was "dull" until they reached Switzerland. There, on Louisa's thirty-third birthday, she met the most tantalizing secret in all her diaries.

Ladislas Wisniewski was Polish, a "very gay & agreeable" eighteen-year-old with a gift for playing sweet airs on the piano. He also had a talent for speaking sweet words to Louisa. According to the December entry of her 1865 diary, there was a "little romance" with "L. W." But was the romance between Laddie and Anna or between Laddie and Louisa?

It is difficult to tell, since Louisa scratched out this part of the entry so forcefully that she left a hole in the paper. Later she wrote the words, "Couldn't be." "Sad times for L. and A.," Louisa scribbled when they left Laddie behind to continue their trip. Then she crossed out the two initials and wrote "all."

The following May, Louisa parted ways with Anna to travel on her own before returning to America. "Feeling as happy as a freed bird," she met Laddie in Paris and spent a "charming" two weeks there. During the day they visited with his Polish friends at cafés and attended the theater. At night he played the piano for her. He called her a Polish phrase meaning "Little Mamma," and she laughingly called him the Polish equivalent of "my darling."

Was Louisa in love with Laddie? She might have been secretly infatuated with the dashing young man in the blue-and-white uniform. Or perhaps he simply brought out the bright side of her "sunshine & shade" personality. At thirty-three, Louisa vowed to her diary not to "grow older in heart as the time goes on." For a few weeks, at least, Laddie made her feel like the young person she had never let herself be. Two years later she immortalized her "whirligig" Laddie as Laurie in *Little Women*.

On returning home, Louisa found her family in good spirits, though Abba's health was failing and they were in debt. With memories of Paris still floating through her mind, she dutifully "fell to work with a will." The effort made her "sick from too hard work," but she wrote twelve potboilers in less than three months to pay the bills.

One of these, "Behind a Mask; or a Woman's Power," is considered among the best of her Gothic thrillers. Both the title and plot explore the idea of deception—a theme in Louisa's own life. Louisa was a woman trying to be a good daughter, who pretended to be A. M. Barnard. In "Behind a Mask" she created an actress posing as a governess who pretended to be a British lady. As in many of Louisa's thrillers, the hero manipulated people until she got what she wanted. If the author behind the mask could not control her personal life, she could make up female characters with "beauty and genius" to do it for her.

Louisa's "rubbishy" tales were as exciting for her as they were for the readers of *Frank Leslie's Illustrated Newspaper*, the popular tabloid that published them. A. M. Barnard managed to keep her secret identity for almost one hundred years. Until 1943, no one but her editor had known that the renowned "Children's Friend" also wrote adult stories that were "dramatic, vivid"—and most unwholesome.

Little Women
• *1866–1868* •

*T*wo years before Louisa was born, Bronson listed six goals in his diary. At the bottom of the list were his marriage, "domestic affairs," and finances. Near the top was an "elementary book"—a moral tale for children. His own writing style was too lofty and convoluted for young people (his diary entries give the impression that he was trying to write a sequel to the Bible). So Bronson did what many parents do: he depended on his offspring to make his own ambition come true.

Bronson engineered Louisa's "Girls' Story" from the start. In September 1857, a publisher asked her to write a girls' book. She tried but complained to her diary that she did not like it. In February 1868, Bronson met with the same publisher. "I spoke of *'The Story for the Girls'* which R. & B.'s asked you to write," he reported to her in a letter. "They want a book of 200 pages or more just as you choose."

His nagging continued. "Father saw Mr. Niles about a fairy book," Louisa told her diary in May 1868. "Mr. N. wants a *girls story,* and I begin 'Little Women.' " Louisa did not enjoy writing the 402-page manuscript and thought it was dull: "Never liked girls or knew many, except my sisters," she complained to her diary.

Why did Louisa write a book that bored her? She must have known how pleased Bronson would be, for she told her diary what *he* had always believed—that "lively, simple books are very much needed for girls." The success of Part I of *Little Women* surprised everyone. "First edition gone and more called for," wrote Louisa in her diary in October 1868. Reviews and letters poured in from readers who found the little women to be so like themselves.

At last, Louisa had won her father's interest and approval. He bragged to his diary about her "superior gifts as a writer" and called her a "dramatic genius." "I am introduced as the father of Little Women," he beamed in his diary, "and am riding in the Chariot of Glory wherever I go."

Since Louisa based *Little Women* on the Alcott family, it seems odd that she allowed Bronson-as-Papa-March to appear so few times. For the first half of the book he was away at war; during the second half he was the "quiet scholar, sitting among his books" while "five energetic women" ran the house.

As if writing with invisible ink, Louisa sneaked a hidden message about her father into the text of *Little Women.* Although Bronson was physically present when she was growing up, she could not depend on him for the necessities of life. Louisa loved the "dear man," but he let her down, year after year. Since she never criticized him aloud, the fictional father's absence disclosed the real father's distance from his family's distress.

While Louisa was writing "Part Second" of *Little Women,* fans pestered her with letters. "Girls write to ask who the little women marry," she wrote in her diary, annoyed, "as if that was the only end and aim of a woman's life." Louisa seemed sure about marriage in her mind. "Liberty is a better husband than love to many of us," she maintained.

Then why did she allow independent Jo to marry at all? Jokingly, she almost called the second part of the book "Leaving the Nest." Perhaps Jo's wedding was an imaginary way for Louisa to separate from the Alcott family. When Jo became engaged in the now-famous scene under the umbrella, she was ready to "walk through life" with Fritz Bhaer, leaving one family to start a new one. Louisa could not leave her family, but Jo could—and did.

Some readers are disappointed that Louisa wed Laurie to Amy instead of Jo. Maybe the author acted out of spite. If she thought she was too old or too duty-bound to marry her "perfect dear," Ladislas (Laurie), then Jo March could not have him either! "I *won't* marry Jo to Laurie to please any one," she grumbled to her dairy.

So Jo married the absentminded Professor Bhaer. He was wise enough to love the *true* Jo, who often "looked far from lovely," sometimes had "a sorrow," and did not always succeed at being good. The enduring message of *Little Women* is not that women have to be perfect for someone to love them, but that they are perfectly lovable as they are.

Louisa showed readers a glimpse of her real self when she inserted a brief lesson toward the end of the book. "Don't laugh at the spinsters, dear girls," she instructed them. "Many silent sacrifices of youth, health, ambition, love itself, make the faded faces beautiful in God's sight." Louisa May Alcott knew all about silent sacrifices. Though *Little Women* was an enormous achievement, writing it exhausted her. There was "no rest," she told her diary in 1869, "for the brains that earn the money."

"Harvest Time"
· *1869–1888* ·

"Twenty years ago, I resolved to make the family independent if I could," Louisa wrote in 1872. "At almost forty that is done. . . . It has cost me my health, perhaps; but as I am still alive, there is more for me to do, I suppose."

The triumph of *Little Women* should have created a more satisfying life for Louisa May Alcott. The income might have given her freedom to explore other writing styles as a playwright or novelist, or the opportunity to pursue her true loves, travel and acting. But real-life happy endings are harder to achieve than made-up ones.

In 1873, Louisa published a book about a working woman called *Work*. This, more than anything else she had written, was "Authentic Alcott." The theme of independence touched women readers trying to earn a living in jobs outside the home. But sales of the book were so low that she went back to writing children's stories, since they made enough money to keep the family "cosey."

Bronson's lecture tours finally became a financial success, and the income from *Little Women* was steady. Yet Louisa was unable to let go of her formulaic series. Over the next twenty years she completed seven more books in the Little Women saga. She wrote hundreds of stories and poems for children, even after her thumb became paralyzed from writing thousands of pages in longhand script. "Never have time to go slowly and do my best," she complained to her diary.

Overwhelmed by her fame as the "Scribbling Spinster" and mobbed as "Miss Ollie" wherever she went, Louisa continued to seek solace in her secret writing. As A. M. Barnard, she produced a few thrilling tales in 1869 and a Gothic novel in 1877. "Enjoyed doing it," she confessed to her diary, "being tired of providing moral pap for the young." The novel also gave her a brief respite from her mother's final illness that same year.

Louisa never recovered her own health after the bout with fever during the Civil War. Like many other nineteenth-century patients, she had been treated with large doses of calomel, or mercury. Doctors then did not understand its toxic nature. She suffered its poisonous effects for the rest of her life: anxiety, weakness, chills, rheumatism, and intestinal disorders. Much of her emotional discontent was due to chronic physical pain.

Yet the mask of duty interfered with happiness too. Louisa had worried about her family for so long that she only knew how to be a caretaker. A fear of debt obsessed her, and she compulsively recorded bills in her diary. In the second-to-last entry written days before her death, she listed a $2.32 payment for milk.

In the twenty years after publication of *Little Women,* Louisa moved eighteen times from Boston to Concord and back again. She even made another trip to Europe. Yet she never settled down in a house of her own. For her, home was with Bronson and Abba, and work was what she did for them, not for herself. Born on her father's birthday, she remained loyal to him till the end. "Come soon," he told her the day before he passed away. Two days later, on March 6, 1888, Louisa May Alcott died of intestinal cancer.

The seeds of separation that she planted in her diaries took root in her thrillers and in *Little Women,* but they never bloomed. Shortly after she finished *Little Women,* she wrote these prophetic words: "I hope success will sweeten me and make me what I long to become more than a great writer, a good daughter." From a distance of over one hundred years we can admire such devotion, yet lament its narrow vision. We know she was a good daughter and beloved children's author. But her adventuresome and imaginative secret writing makes us wonder if she could have been much more.

. . . . .

"A Woman of Character"

Salem, Massachusetts
· *1853–1857* ·

Fifteen-year-old Charlotte Forten had never felt so blue. It was hard for her to leave her father, his second wife, and their sons to move to Salem, Massachusetts, in 1853. But Robert Forten insisted that a free black girl would get a better education in New England than in Philadelphia, and he was right. Though slavery was illegal in Pennsylvania, discrimination was customary—train cars were segregated, and several ice cream "saloons" refused to serve Charlotte.

Still, the serious girl with brooding eyes and aquiline features craved family affection. Her "dear lost mother" had died of tuberculosis when she was three. And when she left Philadelphia, she also left behind aunts, uncles, cousins, and a cherished grandmother. They were all members of the influential Forten family—abolitionists who, beginning with her grandfather, James, worked tirelessly to end slavery.

Even though she lived with another black abolitionist family in Salem, sometimes Charlotte felt like an orphan. Six months after arriving, she began a diary that she called a journal. For the next ten years the plain brown notebooks

were her family. When racial prejudice made the young
woman indignant, her diary-father took her side. If she was
blue, the diary-brother listened. And like an affectionate
sister, the diaries eased Charlotte's loneliness.

She had no real friends at school—white girls who were
"thoroughly kind and cordial" in the classroom refused to
speak to her on the street. Their rejection hurt. She once
flatly noted, "Valentine's Day; but no one has remembered
me." By September of 1854, Charlotte desperately missed her
father and his family. One warm night, with only the moonlight and crickets for company, she wrote:

> I imagine myself again sitting with father and
> [step]mother in our pleasant porch, listening to
> the merry voices of my dear little [half]brothers;
> and a delightful sensation of HOME steals over me.
> But it is only a dream. Good Night! dear friends.
> Pleasant dreams to you!

The diary was no substitute for home, but it helped Charlotte span the miles in her mind. By pretending to talk to her
family in the diary, she felt a little less alone. The diary also let
Charlotte supervise herself, just as a watchful mother would
do. "It will doubtless enable me to judge correctly of the
growth and improvement of my mind from year to year," she
solemnly predicted on the first page.

There were numerous rules of behavior for a proper young
lady in the nineteenth century. Since Charlotte had no parents to scold her, writing in a diary helped her keep those
rules. Brought up with impeccable manners, she was usually
as polite with her diary as with a visitor in the parlor. "Miss

Coffin seems good-natured but not particularly cordial," she tactfully wrote about a new acquaintance.

But when the pressure to be good was too much to bear, the diary let her be a bad girl. Sweet Charlotte also knew the sour taste of jealousy: "T. is pretty, but does not look like a person of much character," she wrote cattily. "I have heard that she is a genius. She does not so impress me."

Charlotte had no parents to remind her that traveling was frowned upon for women, yet her diary shows she understood that restriction quite well. One of her favorite activities was looking at books illustrated with engravings of faraway places. She curtailed visits to the library to look at the pictures, however. Since travel was limited for most women, it was better to avoid books that made her burn with a "foreign fever." The entry shows that Charlotte had learned a crucial domestic lesson: Young women should stay at home.

The studious girl thrived on scholarship. Books let her imagine the larger world beyond women's traditional sphere of home and hearth. Privately tutored as a child in Philadelphia, she spent much of her time in Salem studying French, German, and Latin, reading European and classical history, and reciting works by the Romantic poets of her day: Longfellow, Wordsworth, Whittier.

And despite her timidity, her diary reveals that she frequently met, conversed, and corresponded with famous figures. She had dinner with journalist William Lloyd Garrison, became friends with poet John Greenleaf Whittier, and wrote to Harriet Martineau, an English reformer. In both Philadelphia and Salem, Charlotte kept company with some of the best minds of the century—all of them abolitionists.

References to slavery drop like tears throughout Charlotte's diary. The trial of Anthony Burns, a fugitive slave who was sent back into slavery by a Massachusetts court, dominates the first week's entries. "I can write no more," Charlotte said in despair when the court ruled against Burns (despite a mob protest in Boston joined by Bronson Alcott). "A cloud seems hanging over me, over all our persecuted race, which nothing can dispel."

Her painful experiences as an African-American made her exquisitely sensitive to the similar plight of others. When she saw American Indians camped in a field, Charlotte expressed an empathy for them that was rare for her time. It made her sad to think of "the great changes that had befallen the sons of the forest since they wandered here."

She understood the loss of those "bold and free possessors of the soil," for grief had settled around her shoulders like an old shawl. When news of the Anthony Burns decision reached her father, he decided he could no longer live in America, even as a free black. He moved his family to Canada, leaving Charlotte behind. She felt deserted.

For years Charlotte couldn't face her mother's death or her father's abandonment, even in her diary. Gradually, though, she brought herself to write about the loss of both parents. Two years after her father left, twenty-year-old Charlotte admitted:

> It is hard for me to bear. To thee, alone, my journal, can I say with tears how very hard it is. I have a loving heart, though some may doubt it, and I long for a parent's love—for the love of my only parent; but it seems denied me; I know not why.

Perhaps if Robert Forten had known what Charlotte's diary knew, he would not have left his only daughter behind without even writing good-bye.

Salem
· *1857–1862* ·

Charlotte graduated twice during her years in Salem—first from a private high school, then from a teacher-training course at what was called a normal school. A melancholy tune plays through the latter entries. Three months after enrolling in normal school, she complained that out of all her companions, only her studies were her "truest friend."

After graduation in 1857, nineteen-year-old Charlotte had no money. Since her father was "utterly unable" to help her, she hoped to earn income by writing, one of the few respectable jobs available to educated women. She pushed herself to write, though she had little confidence in her ability. "Determined to finish my story . . . it seems to *me* silly and flat," she wrote in 1857. "I can't see any sense in it. Yet *necessity* compels me to try to publish it."

Though her story, "The Lost Bride," was rejected by *Ladies' Home Journal,* some of her essays, a few poems, and a translation of a French novel were published during the 1860s—the same decade when she kept most of her diaries. A high moral tone was expected of a female author in the nineteenth century, so Charlotte's stiff poems and preachy essays drip with biblical *whither*'s, *hither*'s, *thee*'s and

thine's. It is her more candid diaries by which we know her as
a writer now.

Unable to make a living by writing, she was relieved when
the town of Salem offered her a teaching job in the middle of
the school year. "Wonderful indeed it is!" she happily noted
in her diary.

But the job was harder than she thought it would be. "The
weather is hot; the children restless," she moaned, "and I find
a teacher's life not nearly as pleasant as a scholar's." She
dragged through the rest of the school year. When classes
began again in the fall, her enthusiasm was broth-thin: "First
day of school. 'Tis pleasant to see the bright young faces
again; but it isn't pleasant to go to work." By the next day, she
felt desperate: "This constant warfare is crushing, killing
me!"

Only Charlotte's diary knew her misery. Nurturing children was a good woman's responsibility—how could she
admit to anyone else that she simply hated the job? Com-
plaining to the diary helped her survive the year, but she
never learned to like the profession.

Perhaps Charlotte's poor health prevented her from enjoy-
ing her students. During a nine-year period she left Salem
four times to recuperate in Philadelphia from respiratory
ailments (where she read Louisa May Alcott's *Hospital
Sketches* with "great interest"). In 1860 she tried a mineral
water "Cure" in Worcester, Massachusetts, and was treated
by an "excellent" doctor named Seth Rogers.

Charlotte grew quite fond of Dr. Rogers. When they met
on social occasions, she carefully noted the event in her diary.
He was only a good friend, she told her diary, but when she

wrote that she had seen him twice in one day for a "delightful drive and talk," the words bubbled with giddy hope.

Raised to be sexually pure before marriage, Charlotte expressed desires in her diary that she couldn't say out loud to anyone. "I long for the pressure of a living hand in mine, the touch of loving lips upon my aching brow," she confessed. She had little hope for such intimacy, though, perhaps because she had such a low opinion of herself: "There is none, for me, and never will be," wrote the young woman whose friends once compared her to a "pretty" Italian princess. "I could only love one whom I could look up to, and reverence and that *one* would never think of such a poor little ignoramus as I."

Like other nineteenth-century young women, Charlotte had been told that marriage was the only path to a woman's fulfillment. She thought her life was already over because there was no special man in her life. Remarkably, she considered herself a "forlorn old maid" at the young age of twenty-two.

St. Helena
• *1862–1863* •

*W*hen Charlotte heard that Union troops had captured the South Carolina Sea Islands in November 1861, she was thrilled—this early Civil War victory might give some purpose to her life! "I wonder why it is that I have this strange feeling of not LIVING OUT MYSELF," she wondered in her diary. "What means this constant restlessness, this longing for something, I know not what?" She was so lonely that she even gave her diary a name. *A.* would be her "cher ami," her "unknown friend."

Since fleeing Confederates on the Sea Islands were forced to leave plantations and slaves behind, the federal government planned to send northern teachers to teach the freed people on the Sea Islands. The assignment would be dangerous, but Charlotte was determined to go. She thought it was her duty as a Christian and a free African-American to teach the former slaves how to read and write.

On October 1862, she was "astonished" to learn that the government had accepted her application to teach on St. Helena Island. Charlotte was unnerved when she realized she had to leave immediately, but she had been busily sewing clothes for a month and was ready for the challenge. "At any cost I *will* go," Charlotte vowed to her diary.

And within a few days, she was at sea. Like most of the northern teachers who went south to teach the freed people, she was seasick on the week-long voyage. "Of all the doleful, dismal, desperate experiences," she complained, "seasickness is certainly the dolefulest, dismalist, desperate-est." But for a young woman who had never been beyond the Northeast, the thrill of travel was a tonic. In two days she found herself sitting on top of a coil of ropes, "*luxuriating* in the glorious beauty of the sea and sky" as she calmly watched a companion vomit for hours over the side of the ship.

Even a nighttime storm didn't bother her. "The vessel rocked and plunged, the planks creaked and groaned; the sea broke upon the boat with thunderous roars," Charlotte cheerfully remembered. She was amazed that she had "two or three most refreshing sleeps in the very height of the storm." When a missing baby was finally found unharmed under a berth where it had rolled during the night, Charlotte was "amused" by the "little episode."

Like clean sea air, a new voice was sweeping through the pages of Charlotte's diary. The girl so full of "shame and sorrow" left those feelings behind as the ship steamed south. She would still suffer from bouts of loneliness on St. Helena, but physical activity, a sense of purpose, and even discomfort ("Oh the *fleas*!!") cured her depression.

When she finally saw St. Helena, she thought she was in a "strange wild dream." The coastal landscape was as flat as a sand dollar. Nothing about it resembled the busy streets of Philadelphia or the rocky soil near her old school in Massachusetts. Most of all, the people were different.

Charlotte's first challenge was to rearrange her expectations about the freed African-Americans on the island. She had packed more than clothes, books, and a diary when she left New England. Her baggage also included stereotypes about the intelligence of former slaves—abolitionists assumed the freed people were so damaged by slavery that learning to read and write would be difficult. And like other Yankee "schoolmarms," Charlotte was hampered by northern inexperience with southern black culture.

She soon grew to love the island countryside with its "large noble trees" and the "long bearded moss" that cloaked every branch. But it took a year to adjust to her fellow black Americans and for them to accept her—a secret she kept from everyone, even her diary.

When Charlotte arrived in South Carolina, she lived with northern white women in "Oaklands," an abandoned plantation house staffed by former slaves accustomed to waiting on white people. The servants were suspicious of her fancy manners and white-sounding speech. Most African-Americans on the Sea Islands had never met a free black person. They questioned whether someone their own color could have authority over them.

We know of her troubles only from others' diaries and letters. "The people on our place are inclined to question a good deal about 'dat brown gal,' as they call Miss Forten," wrote one of Charlotte's coworkers, Laura Towne, in her diary. "Aunt Becky required some coaxing to wait upon her and do her room. Aunt Phyllis is especially severe in the tone of her questions. I hope they will respect her."

The freed women thought that serving Charlotte meant a drop in their own status. And they must have sensed that she considered them strange. In a letter to abolitionist William Lloyd Garrison she admired the women's "natural courtesy of manner," but she was secretly frustrated by their language. One woman, she wrote in her diary, had African parents and "speaks a VERY foreign tongue."

In her diary Charlotte referred to the black residents of Oaklands as "these people" and poked fun at their names. "We have ROSE for our little maid-of-all-work, AMORETTA for cook, washer, and ironer, and CUPID, yes Cupid himself, for clerk, oysterman, and future coachman." And she described a wedding as laughable: "T'was amusing to see some of the headdresses. One, of tattered flowers and ribbons, was very ridiculous."

The culture seemed strange to Charlotte, but with her diary to absorb the initial shock, she was finally able to claim "these people" as her people, too. Music provided the bridge. Before coming to St. Helena, old "Scotch Airs" were "special favorites" because her father had sung them to her as a child. But on her first night in South Carolina, she was moved when black boatmen sang "Roll, Jordan, Roll" as they rowed her from ship to dry land. "Their singing impressed me much," she told *A*. "It was so sweet and strange and solemn."

Within six months, Charlotte was drawn irresistibly into the black culture that surrounded her. One day she found herself "in a dark corner of the Praise House," practicing the same shuffling dance steps as the freed people who were having a "shout." "It is perfect time the people keep with hands, feet, and indeed with every part of the body," wrote Charlotte in delight. Because *A*. let her change her mind, she gradually evolved from a critic of Sea Island culture to an appreciative participant.

And the people at Oaklands grew to love Charlotte after discovering that she too was a talented musician. "When they heard her *play on the piano*," an army officer reported in a letter, "it quite put them down, and soon all grew fond of her. Miss Towne says 'she is *the* pet and belle of the island.' "

One morning soon after her arrival, Charlotte left Oaklands to walk the half-mile to school. As she wandered down a sandy lane through the luminous morning light, she worried about her first day of teaching. Some of her pupils had to walk miles to reach the brick church where classes were held. Would they be too tired to learn their lessons?

When the big bell sounded, the children scampered into the church and took their seats on long benches. They were eager and so was she—perhaps her day would be a satisfying one, after all. But that afternoon she trudged wearily back through the scarlet woods and unburdened her troubles to

A.: "Had my first regular teaching experiences, and to you and you only friend beloved, will acknowledge that it was NOT a pleasant one."

It's no wonder that Charlotte was discouraged. Like many teachers of the freed children, she had to cope with an ever-changing number of pupils of all ages and levels: "Had a perfectly IMMENSE school to-day," she wrote. "147, of whom I had 58, at least two-thirds of whom were tiny A-B-C people." And after "dreadfully wearying" days at school, she and her two coworkers taught adults at night. When night class was over, they visited the quarters to nurse children with whooping cough or to mourn those who had died of this often fatal childhood disease.

Despite the difficulties, Charlotte had exciting, sometimes hilarious adventures that she gleefully recounted for *A.*'s "especial benefit." On a food-finding expedition to an abandoned plantation, she was carried triumphantly across a tidal marsh in an old bathtub by "four stout sailors." She told *A.* about meeting runaway slaves from the mainland who stole a boat from their master, then sunk it each night until they could make a perilous nighttime escape to the islands.

She even became friends with Colonel Robert Gould Shaw, who led the first black Union troops, the 54th Massachusetts regiment. He liked Charlotte so well after they had tea that he put her in charge of his three prized horses in case he was killed in battle.

Charlotte Forten's time on the Sea Islands changed her. For years she had lived safely within the pages of her diary—a submissive girl full of "self-contempt." At the same time, the diary had prepared her well for her Sea Island adventure. In its pages, she learned to risk new thoughts and explore different feelings. One emotion was so forbidden, though, that she could not openly admit it to anyone, even *A.*

St. Helena

• *1863–1864* •

Charlotte loved to sleep late, but New Year's Day, 1863, was so important that she crawled out of bed early. That night she filled page after page of her diary with neat script as she described what had been "the most glorious day this nation has yet seen, *I* think." Finally she had realized her vision of freedom for her enslaved race. The Emancipation Proclamation took effect on January 1, and the slaves were officially free.

Like everyone else on the Sea Islands, white and black, Charlotte went by boat to join the celebration on the mainland. As she stepped onto the long wooden dock in Beaufort, she thought she was in a dream. She felt a hand take hers and a "well known voice" speak her name. It was Seth Rogers, her "dear noble friend" from Massachusetts, now a doctor for the Union army.

Charlotte was ecstatic. "I cannot tell you, dear *A.*, how delighted I was to see him; how *good* it was to see the face of a friend from the North, and *such* a friend." They spent the special day together, sharing tears during the moving speeches and laughter at the "merry, delightful dinner" with Colonel Shaw.

When the ship arrived that evening to take her back to St. Helena, she hated to say good-bye to "Dr. R." Later, she fretted over his health. "I fear the exposure of a camp life," she wrote. "Am glad to see that he has warm robes and blankets, to keep him comfortable." Charlotte sounded like a worried spouse, but she could never be married to Dr. Rogers—he already had a wife in the North, and he was white.

Before the week was over, the doctor visited Charlotte at Oaklands. Proudly she bragged, "He came on purpose to see me." Charlotte had little experience with romantic relationships. She may not have realized that she was growing too fond of the married doctor, who obviously enjoyed her company.

But he realized that their attachment was a hazardous one. She naively told *A.* about their next conversation: "The kind, loving words he spoke to me to-night sank deep into my heart. 'As a brother,' he told me to consider him. And I will gladly do so." She ended the entry by taking the innocent role of a child: "He was in full uniform to-day. Makes a splendid looking officer. I looked at him and his horse with childish admiration."

Consciences thus soothed, Charlotte and the doctor continued to see each other. He walked her to school the next day and told her he wished they lived nearer so he could come read to her sometime. She maintained the illusion of friendship in her diary: "Ah! wldn't I enjoy that, unspeakably. It is too bad that I can see so seldom the only old friend I have here,—and such a friend!"

In romantic prose she told "dear A." about their ride at sunset. It was "just he and I," she wrote. "The young moon— just a silver bow—had a singular, almost violet tinge and all around it in the heavens was a rosy glow." The doctor returned Charlotte's affection, telling her how much he cared for her. "It is very pleasant," she wrote, "although I KNOW he thinks far better of me than I deserve."

And one night he sent a note with "a little friend, whose name I am not to mention. But it is a beautiful and true friend." Perhaps this was a photograph of Dr. Rogers, or a freshly picked flower. We'll never know, since Charlotte obeyed the doctor's wishes. She did not reveal the nature of the "friend," not even to trustworthy *A.*

It's unlikely that Seth Rogers and Charlotte Forten ever expressed more than deep friendship to each other. Honor and duty were too important to both of them. In truth, his married state may have allowed them to enjoy each other's company without worry. Had he been single, they would have had to face the possibility of an interracial marriage, which was illegal in most of the United States.

Charlotte's poor health finally brought their pleasant months together to an end. "I have found my strength "steadily decreasing," she wrote in July 1863, "and have been every day tortured by a severe headache." Her "good" doctor advised her to go north, and she sailed to Philadelphia at the end of July.

She returned to St. Helena for seven months, but after her father died of typhoid fever in the spring of 1864, Charlotte left the Sea Islands for good. She mentioned Dr. Rogers several more times in her diary, but their separation may have helped them remember that he was, after all, a married man.

The last diary that Charlotte kept as a young woman ends in May 1864. In June and July 1864, her essays "Life on the Sea Islands, Parts I and II" appeared in *Atlantic Monthly* magazine. Products of her Sea Island diaries, the essays contain much of the same information. The diaries filtered her public writing: Charlotte, the diarist, kept unhappy memories buried as Charlotte, the essayist, presented her best face to the literary world.

For instance, the "motley assemblage" of black soldiers who stood on the wharf the night she first arrived in South Carolina appear in both essay and diary. But the phrase "the most dismal specimens I ever saw" magically disappeared from the published version. Charlotte must have thought she would seem disloyal to her race, as well as unchristian, if she included that candid description in a national magazine.

She did admit to the *Atlantic Monthly* readers that the first day of school was "rather trying." Yet she twisted the facts so she would appear to be a perfect teacher. "After some days of positive, though not severe treatment," she claimed, "order was brought out of chaos, and I found but little difficulty in managing and quieting the tiniest and most restless spirits."

Only her diary knew about her *real* progress after two weeks of teaching: "Had a dreadfully wearying day in school, of which the less said the better." Charlotte's diaries helped her remember her years on St. Helena. They also helped her conceal negative feelings that wouldn't have been acceptable from a good woman.

The works of well-known writers appeared in the same issue as Charlotte's Sea Island essays: Harriet Beecher Stowe, Robert Browning, Henry Longfellow. Had Charlotte been as honest in her public writing as she was in her diary, she might be as well remembered as they are today. Instead, she picked the usual bouquet from a nineteenth-century woman's narrow garden—marriage, motherhood, and religion.

Washington, D. C.

• 1885–1889 •

The 1870s brought more change to Charlotte's life, though we have no diary entries to show how she changed from a delicate young teacher into a stalwart Presbyterian missionary. She taught briefly in Boston, Charleston, and Washington, D.C., but gave up teaching because she continued to "suffer dreadfully" from headaches that she feared were a sign of insanity.

In 1878, forty-one-year-old Charlotte married the Reverend Francis Grimké, a former slave educated in law and theology. Twenty-eight-year-old Francis was twelve years younger than his darling "Lottie," but they were devoted to each other and well matched in intellect and interest. While he campaigned tirelessly for black civil rights from his pulpit, Charlotte wrote letters and essays supporting his position. She also helped found the National Association of Colored Women in 1896, along with Ida B. Wells and Alice Dunbar-Nelson.

Charlotte Forten, who was certain as a girl that she would die before turning twenty, lived to be seventy-six. A bedridden invalid for the last thirteen months of her life, she died of a cerebral embolism in 1914.

The obituary that Francis Grimké wrote for his wife reveals the qualities that were most valued in women during Charlotte's day. She was "sweet and gentle, and yet she was a woman of great strength and character," he wrote. "She was always thoughtful, always considerate for others, never allowing the thought of self to intrude or to interfere with the comfort and happiness of others." Charlotte did live a life of unselfish service, perhaps because she could hide the needs of her other "self" in a diary.

Under an almost saintly exterior, occasional rebellion flared: "Went to church and was victimized with one of Mr. Phillips' dull sermons," she once wrote about a tiresome minister. Charlotte was tranquil on the outside, but her diary knew she was secretly insecure: "I can only tell *you* about my UNskilfulness," she wrote. "OF COURSE we lost our way coming back, and I in trying to turn the horse, ran up against a tree. All this I tell you dear *A.* as a great secret!"

Most important to the ideal of a perfect woman, only her diary understood her attachment to a married man. There was a "magnetism about him," she wrote about Seth Rogers, that was "impossible to resist." Charlotte Forten's secret writing made it possible for her to express her love, yet keep her purity—the quality valued most of all in a good nineteenth-century woman.

SARAH JANE FOSTER

· · · · ·

"Soldier of Light and Love"

❧

Martinsburg, West Virginia
· *November 1865 – January 1866* ·

*W*hile Charlotte Forten was teaching in South Carolina, twenty-six-year-old Sarah Jane Foster was cleaning houses in her hometown of Gray, Maine. The work was honest, but Sarah was like a character in a story she wrote in 1865—"tied down to an irksome drudgery, kept back from all improvement, growing worse day by day." Sarah was the self-educated daughter of a shoemaker. One of seven children, the young woman with a moon-shaped face and determined mouth meant to have a better life than her parents had. And she expected to find that life as a single woman.

In November 1865, seven months after the end of the Civil War, adventuresome Sarah took charge of her life. She gratefully exchanged her bucket and scrub brush for the primitive conditions of a "small basement" school in Martinsburg, West Virginia. Although missionary teachers were paid only a pittance (she couldn't even afford to buy winter boots), she thought that teaching was the quickest route to improving herself.

Sarah was like hundreds of other northern women called "Soldiers of Light and Love" by the missionary organizations that sponsored them—she believed it was her Christian duty to go south to help the freed people. Within four months after arriving in Martinsburg, West Virginia, she had a day school of seventy children, taught over thirty adults for four nights a week, and held weekly Sunday school meetings. She should have been exhausted, but compared with cleaning houses, this work was exhilarating!

In a letter to *Zion's Advocate,* a Baptist newspaper in Portland, Maine, Sarah reported she was in the schoolroom over forty-two hours a week. "Yet I am wonderfully sustained," she wrote. The young teacher tasted success twice— once with the children and again when she wrote in her diary that teaching "gave life such a zest."

Twenty-three-year-old Sarah had no training as a teacher, but she had a bonnetful of common sense. She could be as hard with her pupils as a Maine winter, then soft as sugar. Her students were "eager to learn" reading, writing, spelling, and arithmetic because she sprinkled them with praise. But if a troublemaker dared to provoke her, she had a strict schoolteacher's stare that could burn holes in his or her head.

Evening school turned out to be the best part of Sarah's teaching day. The adults came from miles around, including a young man who was especially smart. Sarah admired her "night scholar," John Brown, from the first chilly November evening they met. A former slave and Union soldier, he had taught himself to read and write. She saw immediately that he was "really very intelligent," a glowing star in her composition class of thirty-six adults.

Soon Sarah thought of John as her partner, not just a pupil. He became her "faithful ally." "I could not have done justice to the evening school without his aid," she wrote to *Zion's Advocate*. "Seeing my dilemma he quietly and unobtrusively took charge of several of the lower classes to the neglect of his own books."

Shyly, a secret began to peek through the lines of Sarah's diary. And as the skein of writing unravels, a surprise appears: Sarah was falling love with the twenty-six-year-old man with dark skin, a "fine, intelligent face," and "curly" hair.

During January 1866, Sarah mentioned John Brown's name in twenty-six out of thirty-one entries. "Had an excellent prayer meeting," she noted early in the month. "Mr. Brown was there too. I shall enjoy the meetings very much." After talking to Mr. Brown about his soul, she wrote ecstatically, "I am *so* happy tonight."

At first, Sarah did not seem to realize the strength of her own feelings. From fixing shutters to teaching a *"perfect"* map lesson, John Brown could do no wrong. More than anything, though, she admired his unassuming ways. "How little he knows his own worth," she marveled. John was "good and quiet," she bragged in her diary, a "modest and unaffected" man.

Falling in love was the last thing that sensible Sarah expected to do when she arrived in "wild and romantic" West Virginia. Already doubtful about the wisdom of marriage for women who "try to rise," she never expected that a freedman would gently claim her heart. Perhaps that is why the hostile residents of Martinsburg—and Sarah's diary—knew about her secret even before she did.

Martinsburg
· *January 1866–April 1866* ·

*S*uspicious rumors about Sarah began during a bitter cold snap in early January. The nights turned "bad and snowy," and she was so concerned about "the little ones" at school that she warmed their small, gloveless hands in hers each morning. While visiting poor families in town, she worried that black and white families alike paid "exorbitant rents" for two-room "wretched little shanties."

After two weeks the snow turned to mud. But as the air temperature rose, so did the tempers of the poor white people. They disapproved of Sarah's visits to black families (she called on John Brown's family twelve times). They were angry that black men escorted her safely home from school each night.

These uneducated people had twice been losers—they had little money and status before the Civil War and almost nothing to call their own when the fighting was over. Homeless, many lived in makeshift shelters that Sarah labeled "droll coops." Now they resented the aid and education being offered to former slaves by the Freedmen's Bureau. As one of Sarah's adult students said, "T'aint them that used to own servants that's so hard on us, but them that never had none."

Violence erupted one Friday evening at the school when

"some rascals" broke down the door. Fearing for Sarah's safety, several of her students, including John Brown, walked her home. She sensed that her troubles weren't over. "Because the work of God has started here," she wrote that night, "Satan has begun to show his power."

Sarah was confused. She had come south to offer friendship and help to the black community. Wouldn't they feel betrayed if she stopped her home visits? Some of the men who walked her home were "seekers of Christ." Wouldn't it be unchristian to refuse their escort?

She turned to the diary for help. After confronting the problem there, she decided to stand firmly loyal to the freed people. When a black man was threatened after escorting her through the streets, she was indignant. "I don't care," she declared to the diary and herself. "If he is not afraid to do it I am not. I shall treat all well who treat me well both black and white."

Even worse, she heard that "some [whites] talked of watching for Mr. Brown too." Sarah scorned the warning. When she saw John in the street on Saturday, she defiantly told her diary that she "stopped to talk, in part to show the street groups that I did not care for them." In her righteous anger, it was hard for her to see the larger picture. Naively, she did not understand that her boldness might put the school, her job, and black lives at risk.

The next Thursday night, violence exploded again. The "roughs" were "terribly exasperated" by her behavior and pounded the school building with clubs. They smashed the door off its hinges with a twenty-pound stone. When black guards fired at the intruders, Sarah instinctively rushed to protect her dear John Brown.

Later that night, sitting alone in her room with the diary, Sarah finally faced her feelings for John. "I misunderstood the firing," she confided, "and caught his hand to hold him back lest he should be shot. I could not help it." John's bravery only deepened Sarah's attachment. "John Brown says that he thinks it is his cross to stay here and stand or fall with those of his color. He is noble." And at last she realized the danger: "God help him," she prayed in her diary.

When some of the "rogues" were arrested, the incidents stopped. Though the crisis was over, Sarah's feelings were more powerful than ever. As winter dragged on, she continued to talk about John to the only friend who could listen. "John was not in. How I miss him when he stays out," she wrote gloomily. She wanted him to have a "white man's chance," to be "educated to help his race."

By now, Sarah knew how she felt about John. Yet she still refused to admit it to her diary. "I heard tonight that I was going to marry John Brown," she reported. "What next? Well let the fools talk. Can't they have wit enough to let me alone?"

Sometimes she seemed to deliberately withhold information from the diary. "I like the Browns of course," she wrote in response to the rumors, "but have given no cause for talk." Perhaps she was afraid that secret words of love written on the narrow pages of her book could be used as a weapon. If her diary fell into the wrong hands, both she and John would be in grave danger, since neither law nor custom allowed interracial marriage.

Because of Sarah's great caution, we will never know the details of her greatest secret. One Friday night in February, she furtively wrote that she had "carried out a wayward purpose." Sarah was convinced that what she had done was right, but she could "hardly dare trust" her diary with the information.

Since she shrouded her actions in mysterious phrases, we can only guess what happened. There may have been a stolen kiss or a lingering embrace that night. Perhaps she finally confessed her love to John on their cold and dark walk home, or even suggested that they make plans to leave Martinsburg together. Whatever Sarah had done, she felt confident about it. "Nature made me wayward and independent," she declared to her diary, "and I must act myself." And she was hopeful about the outcome: "I think all is for the best."

Still, she was nervous when she saw John at Sunday school the following day. "I felt anxious to hear what came of my freak," she wrote in veiled words the next evening, "but felt well prepared for what came." The puzzle of what happened will never be solved, though we know she still felt trapped by strong emotion: "I am relieved and yet more ensnared than ever."

Had John rejected her offer of love or urged her to be more cautious? If so, she had her work to keep her from "sad and discouraging fancies" about him. In a strict voice, she promised her diary to use "prayer and self denial" to save souls.

Teaching and religious duties did help Sarah, but her feelings for John remained as deep as ever. In March she called him her "*best friend*," using underlined words that shimmer with secrecy. And in April she wrote, "He is *so* good—*so* noble. Oh Lord answer thou my prayers."

Sarah was so devoted to John and her pupils that she did not want to leave in July for a summer break—"I am in love with my work," she declared. So when she heard a rumor that she might be leaving even earlier, she was distraught.

"I am as innocent as a babe unborn and I cannot bear to think of a change," she wrote. But the hearsay was true. Because of the racial "incidents," the Freedmen's Bureau insisted that Sarah's supervisor, Reverend Brackett, transfer her to a school in Harper's Ferry, West Virginia. Heartbroken, Sarah wanted to leave Martinsburg right away, then decided that "resignation" was "better than rebellion."

White Martinsburg after the Civil War was like a parched forest in a drought. Poverty, hunger, and humiliation were ready to ignite, and Sarah had been the match. How easy it was to blame a "wayward" woman for the fire. She had tried her best to be the ideal woman who made everyone around her happy, but there were simply too many people to please. Her supervisor wanted a docile teacher who would stay out of trouble. The local agent for the Freedmen's Bureau demanded a sympathetic northern woman who would act like a southerner. The black families needed her help and encouragement, and the white folks did not want her at all.

Sarah rebelled at her unfair treatment. In a conversation with the Freedmen's Bureau agent she was "rough, not to say rude." After receiving a lecture from Mr. Brackett, though, she agreed to apologize. Then a voice of authority took over the writing in her diary, as she prayed to "conquer self at once."

Like other women, Sarah had probably heard many real voices—parents, relatives, ministers—remind her that a woman should be quiet and submissive. When she couldn't conform, their voices spoke again through her diary, telling her to obey. But no nineteenth-century woman could ever reach the impossible goals expected of her. Like climbing a mountain of sand, the top—perfection—was always out of reach.

Harper's Ferry, West Virginia
· April 1866–June 1866 ·

Leaving Martinsburg made Sarah so mad that she cried every time she thought about it. Then the lump in her throat turned into a small, hard stone. In one of her letters to *Zion's Advocate,* she openly disagreed with the transfer. I believe that "the change is not wise, and that time will prove it so," she announced. When she lied, "Of course I submit quietly," she could deceive the readers of the paper because her diary had heard the truth: "I am foolish to feel so," she admitted in private, "but I cannot get reconciled to the change."

Worst of all, she missed the company of her dear John Brown. Each night as she fell asleep, she wished she were at a

Martinsburg prayer meeting. And when she wondered in her diary if she would ever get married, there was a glint of promise in the words. "As for me, God only knows. *I* know what I hope, and I must 'wait and see.' "

Though Sarah was lonely and depressed, she slowly adjusted to the new school in Harper's Ferry. After three weeks she finally got a "noble" letter from John. Nervous about seeming too forward, she wrote to him, then destroyed the letter. Taught that a perfect woman was a flower on a stem, she waited impatiently to be picked by the man she loved.

Yet independent Sarah found it hard to stay passive. She decided to visit Martinsburg. "I've great hopes of a good time . . . hope he'll be at home Sunday at least." With the aid of her diary, her broken spirit was beginning to mend— the simple act of writing the word *hope* cheered her. She did meet John at church on Sunday, and he gave her his picture when they visited again on Monday morning. "I shall ever love the colored people of Martinsburg," she promised herself, "especially the noble Brown family."

On a cool Thursday at the end of June 1866, twenty-seven-year-old Sarah "made lots of goodbyes," received a "nice letter" from John Brown, and packed her bags. The next day she left to return to Maine for the summer. She admitted she did not feel as homesick as the rest of the northern teachers. "I love my work better I think," she explained to her diary.

Sharing her troubles with the diary had helped her survive a difficult, dangerous year, and she already looked forward to returning in the fall. But Sarah Jane never saw the misty hills of West Virginia again.

Gray, Maine
• *June 1866 – August 1867* •

$\mathcal{S}$arah was as blue as the ink in her diary when she got a letter from the Home Mission Society. She knew she had done nothing wrong, but because of the trouble, the society accused her of creating the *"very appearance of evil."* Her teaching commission was not renewed for the next year.

She must have been even sadder when she got a letter from John Brown's sister. He had been forced to leave his family in Martinsburg to find work in a nearby town. Although a sea journey of six hundred miles separated them, John and Sarah were still close in spirit.

They seemed to have made plans that she shared with her family. "I said a few words about what John Brown and I have been talking about," Sarah told her diary. "It seemed to be the best. Now I have dropped the matter."

Maybe they intended for John to move to Maine, where an interracial marriage would have been difficult but not impossible. Sarah knew that life might be easier in Maine for an African-American man. He could even go to Bates College, a Freewill Baptist school nearby, in Lewiston. "The people here have no prejudice against color," she recorded. "I have their full sympathy."

Yet sometimes Sarah seemed opposed to marriage for herself. She sorted out her uncertain feelings in the diary. "I could not marry for such a destiny," she vowed. She did not think she would ever marry, "not now nor very soon." Although society exalted marriage and motherhood as the ideal states for nineteenth-century women, Sarah thought the lives of the married women in town were as dreary as December. They were "mere domestic drudges" who sat all day weaving cloth for the local mill. She was afraid that an endless round of babies, housework, and mill work would tie her to a life like theirs.

Sarah was realistic about class distinctions. She did not aspire to the empty "chivalry" of the southern "aristocracy" who had refused to board northern teachers in West Virginia. Yet she understood that continued reading and self-education might help her "rise," just as it helped her sister and brother who had entered the medical profession.

Writing might also help her "rise." Before moving to West Virginia, she had published three morally correct stories in *Home Monthly,* a "family fireside" magazine. The tales featured pious female heroines—an orphan girl, a "crippled" child, a "worn and weary" teacher. Sarah's cardboard characters and gooey plots now seem as sentimental as a greeting card, but they were typical of the domestic fiction that filled nineteenth-century women's magazines.

Before she could submit any more stories for publication, the American Missionary Association offered her a teaching job in the fall of 1867. News about the racial incidents in Martinsburg had traveled to the association, but they were willing to take advantage of her considerable teaching skills.

In a callous attempt to control her behavior, they assigned her to an isolated farm near Charleston, South Carolina. Ironically, their punishment was a reward for self-reliant Sarah Jane, who looked forward "to a period of independent enjoyment."

Charleston, South Carolina
• *October 1867–June 1868* •

Like Charlotte Forten, Sarah found the South Carolina coast to be so different from New England that she could hardly describe it: "I cannot picture by words this place, bordered with trees, fringed with long grey atmospheric moss," she wrote in a letter to *Zion's Advocate,* "but can only assure you that it is very pretty and pleasant."

She held classes for freed children in a tiny chapel on a farm run by an African-American couple. Sarah did not care that she had "no white neighbors at all," for the man and his wife were "excellent people." After the troubles in West Virginia, she welcomed their warm hospitality.

She was as surprised as Charlotte had been by the cold winter in South Carolina and kept a woodstove burning in the schoolroom—the boys and girls carried bundles of firewood balanced on their heads, a custom brought by their ancestors from Africa. And like Charlotte, Sarah was fascinated by African-American religious services. The "musical tide" of singing reminded her of a "powerful torrent pouring over a rocky bed."

Many of her pupils had to quit school in early spring to help parents in the fields. At the end of the 1868 school year Sarah had only thirty-six students, but she was content. "My school yet goes happily on," she wrote, "and I almost dread to leave." Wherever Sarah went, she made a home for herself—now she had to say good-bye again to an African-American community she had grown to love.

It was especially hard to think about chilly Maine when it was "fully summer now" in Charleston. Blackberries, green peas, and roses "as thick as the sand flies" made Sarah reluctant to face another voyage home. She had a scheme, though, that would make the trip worthwhile.

She requested that the Missionary Association allow her to make a stop in Baltimore, Maryland, "as I desire to make a short trip westward." Sarah must have longed to visit her old friends in Martinsburg, especially John Brown. She had to give up the plan, however, after agreeing to take three orphaned girls to New York. That may have been for the best, since she might not have heard the news about John—he had married a woman named Hannah sometime in 1867.

The trip home was not perfect—there may have been the usual seasickness—and though Sarah was usually in "excellent health," she developed a headache in New York. By the time she reached Maine, she had a "severe cold." But within a few days she felt "finely rested" and wrote a long, newsy letter to *Zion's Advocate*.

The letter described a peculiar incident during her last

prayer meeting in South Carolina. A black preacher had suddenly turned to her in the middle of his sermon. "Tain't likely that we'll ever meet again in this world," he said, "but I'll pray for you ma'am, I'll pray for you, and God haint never refused me anything that I've asked in faith for these thirty-six years."

Sarah was "deeply touched" but puzzled, for she knew she would see the man again. Already she had found a nearby location for a school when she returned in the fall. Unlike some of the northern teachers, Sarah itched to get back to her job. "I miss them now," Sarah said of her pupils in her last letter to *Zion's Advocate*, "and would like to have them again in charge."

These were twenty-nine-year-old Sarah's last words to the newspaper. The next night she "passed from the scenes of earth," according to a July 1, 1868 obituary in *Zion's Advocate*. While in South Carolina she had contracted yellow fever, the same disease that had killed so many African-Americans in that swampy low country.

As a teacher for the freed people, Sarah Jane Foster shared some of the qualities of the mythical model woman— nurture, piety, self-sacrifice (she even gave her life). She presented this side of herself to the Baptist readers of *Zion's Advocate*. For them she painted the picture of a patient, kind woman who was obedient to the wishes of supervisor, church, and God.

Yet Sarah's diary shows another person hiding behind that unfinished portrait. A plucky young woman, she traveled when women were supposed to stay at home. With little help from other whites, she bravely fought for black civil rights.

And her open, generous nature allowed her to risk a forbidden love. As hard times tested Sarah Jane Foster, her diary gave her a heart and mind of her own. Never able to completely escape, she still managed to rattle the doors and windows of nineteenth-century woman's domestic cell.

"A Lady Most Foolish"

St. Louis, Missouri
· 1857–1867 ·

Sausage curls swinging, seven-year-old Kate O'Flaherty scrambled up the cherry tree. She looked over at her pug-nosed friend, Kitty, in the opposite bough and grabbed the branch above like a monkey. Kate was already recklessly high in the tree, but that was the point. A daredevil in pantalets, she loved the thrill of taking a risk.

Kate's passionate spirit came from the three women who raised her: A French Creole great-grandmother, grandmother, and mother. Her Irish Catholic father died when she was five, so the Creole culture of her female relatives provided the spice of her childhood years. Her great-grandmother conversed with her in Creole French, supervised daily piano lessons, and taught her to "face all questions coolly and fearlessly." Best of all, she entertained little Kate with risqué anecdotes about her notorious ancestors. Family lore about adultery and interracial marriage was not typical fare for most middle-class girls, but it whetted Kate's appetite for taboo topics.

At an early age, then, Kate learned Creole gaiety, Irish humor, French manners, Catholic morals, and southern loyalty—all while growing up in St. Louis, Missouri, a rough-and-tumble American town. Kate's unusual childhood left her with a taste for the daring and the different. It also gave her the capacity for intense emotions. Now what would she do with all of them?

Like a river in spring, young Kate's heart often spilled over with feeling. She could hardly bear the beauty of the piano music she played for Kitty—each chord sounded too perfect for this imperfect world. And she loved books—the fairy tales that made her giggle, the romances that brought on a swoon. Even the hilarity of playing charades seemed too exquisite to stand.

Many of these emotional escapades took place at Kitty's house, where Kate often spent the night—a rare freedom for well-bred little girls in St. Louis. It was there that Kate made her greatest discovery. When the two friends' pet bird died, they tenderly buried it in the garden, and Kate wrote her first piece of literature: an epitaph that she read over the bird's fresh grave. For the first time, Kate O'Flaherty realized that written words could express her deepest feelings.

After growing up, she used the discovery to write over one hundred short stories and a novel as shocking as the tales she heard at her great-grandmother's knee: *The Awakening*. The book tarnished Kate's reputation, but during the renaissance of women's literature in the 1960s, it brought her literary fame. First published in 1899, this classic novel of secret longing still speaks to readers today who question women's role in society. The main character of the book resembles

Kate: She is a keeper of rules on the outside, but a tempestuous creature within.

As a child, Kate felt fine about *some* of her feelings—girls in her day were free to express religious, nostalgic, or romantic sentiments. The scrapbook she kept when she was ten was a public record of such approved emotions. Gold words engraved on the cover, "Leaves of Affection," dictated the contents: Kate crammed the tan book with pious holy cards and sentimental pictures, and she let friends write romantic poetry on its multicolored pages.

But she needed another place to deposit her anger, annoyance, boredom, grief, and loneliness. Public display of these feelings was not encouraged at the Sacred Heart Academy boarding school in St. Louis, where she was a sometime student until her graduation in 1868. The school rules must have seemed terribly confining after the freedom of home. A code of behavior governed every moment of every day, even sleeping. A girl could not sleep curled up, the nuns decreed, but had to lie flat on her back with hands crossed on her chest "like a Christian."

Kate found little ways to resist the rules, though. During holy Mass, as candles flickered and a curtain of incense hung solemnly in the air, she slipped amusing notes to friends farther down the pew. And toward the end of her years at Sacred Heart, she wrote notes to herself—in a diary.

St. Louis
· *1867–1870* ·

*K*ate's second album, titled "Katie O'Flaherty, St. Louis, 1867," was still a semipublic document. Originally meant to be a "copybook," teachers checked it to make sure she had copied long passages from literature. She also let friends read entries—they later commented on her "remarkable" writing ability. Even so, this diary became sixteen-year-old Kate's secret escape passage to her private thoughts.

In one of her first entries, she rescued herself from pent-up grief by writing an essay called "The Early Dead." Death visited her house often when she was growing up. A train accident took her father, then her beloved great-grandmother died when Kate was thirteen. She lost one brother to drowning and another during the Civil War that split the country and her childhood in half between 1861 and 1865. After the war started, even Kitty moved away, and Kate did not know if she would ever see her best friend again (Kitty did return in 1868).

Kate was especially lonely when she graduated from high school in 1868. She had no sisters or brothers, and the prewar closeness with Kitty had vanished. The black-and-green speckled diary became Kate's "very entertaining" friend. Of course, it was Kate's own thoughts that were so amusing. "What a dear good confidant my book is," she wrote. "If it does not clear my doubts, at least it does not contradict and oppose my opinions."

The diary was also a way for Kate to go to confession without doing penance for sins. No priest ever heard the unchristian complaints she made about a dreary trip to New Orleans with her mother, a child, an invalid, and two of her mother's friends—a "giggler" and a "walking breathing nonentity." Kate, who loved "brightness and gaiety and life and sunshine," was miserable. No one but her diary heard that the trip was "not remarkably gay."

And Kate's diary entries hid her silent rebellion against St. Louis high society during her social debut, or "coming out" season. The beginning of a lifelong weariness with the social game shows in this entry:

> What a nuisance all this is—I wish it were over. I write in my book for the first time in months; parties, operas, concerts, skating and amusements *ad infinitum* have so taken up my time that my dear reading and writing that I love so well have suffered much neglect.

Eighteen-year-old Kate was a puzzle, even to herself. She told her diary she was a "creature who loves amusements," yet the shallowness of debutante dances disgusted her. "I am invited to a ball and I go. I dance with people I despise; amuse myself with men whose only talent lies in their feet."

With her thick wavy hair, deep-set eyes, and gift for hilarious mimicry, she had many friends of both sexes. But in her diary she poked fun at her peers. With sharp humor, she described the art of making conversation with a self-centered man:

> All that is required of you is to have control over the muscles of your face—to look pleased and chagrined and surprised, indignant, and under every circumstance—interested and entertained. Lead your antagonist to talk about himself. He will not enter reluctantly upon the subject, I assure you—and twenty to one—he will report you as one of the most entertaining and intelligent persons, although the whole extent of your conversation was but an occasional "What did *you* say?"— "What did *you* do?"—"What do *you* think?"

Kate looked to her diary for a willing ear. "You are the only one, my book," she told her companion, "with whom I take the liberty of talking about myself." When she was nineteen, though, she found a new comrade and did not breathe a word of it to the diary. She shut her old friend away in a "great immense chest," burying it under piles of heavy books until she needed it again.

A year later, in May 1870, she was frank in her reunion with her younger self. "I—have not missed it," she wrote. "Pardon me, my friend, but I never flatter you." Then she announced her grand secret: In two weeks, she would marry. Kate did not tell the diary how she met "the right man," or even his name. No one had known about their courtship.

"And how surprised every one was," she gloated, "for I had kept it so secret."

During her year away from the diary, the flow of Kate's emotion had been too deep and swift to contain with written words. She wanted to be swept away by romance, not reflect on it. But she did share the nervous flutter of her wedding day. "The whole day seems like a dream to me now," she wrote. "Went to church and found myself married before I could think what I was doing." Kate described a lovely time with champagne and much "kissing of old and young." And finally, she introduced her diary to her beloved husband: Oscar Chopin.

The Honeymoon Diary
• June 1870 – September 1870 •

Twenty-year-old Kate turned the second half of her copybook into a honeymoon diary. She wrote in it regularly as she and Oscar wound their way by train through Europe, though some feelings were too embarrassing to share, even with a diary. She only hinted at wedded bliss, since women in her time were not supposed to admit to the same sexual feelings as men. "It was a *lovely* night!" she vaguely described her wedding night. Too shy to write about married love, she wrote passionate phrases about music instead: An orchestra was her "chief pleasure," and she loved church organ music that sounded like a storm.

Then she discovered another passion: solitude. After a month of traveling, Kate set out one day to walk through the streets of Zurich, Switzerland, while Oscar napped. Restrictive clothing made sports impossible, so middle-class young women in Kate's day walked for exercise. They were usually accompanied by someone else, though, as if they were children. Kate gloried in the delicious freedom of her solitary walk.

"How very far I *did* go," she said in wonderment to her diary. A glass of beer at a "friendly little beer garden" and a smuggled cigarette made the escape even more delightful. Such vices were forbidden to women, not because they were harmful, but because they were unladylike.

Still, Kate found it difficult to be a full-fledged rebel. When she skipped Mass, she felt a twinge of guilt and had to confess to the diary/priest: "Sunday! *Intended* to go to church." And when she had a chance to gamble, she lost all nerve. "I was tempted to put down a silver piece myself," she wrote, "but had not the courage." Sometimes Kate could defy the code of proper behavior for women, and sometimes she could only imagine it. Either way, her diary cheered her on.

New Orleans

• *1870–1879* •

*W*hen the honeymoon was over, Kate and Oscar moved to New Orleans, Louisiana, where Oscar became a cotton merchant and twenty-year-old Kate became a mother. In the nineteenth century, pregnant women were supposed to hide their condition, not flaunt it in public. But Kate cherished her independent walks too much to conform. Her diary became her accomplice. In its pages, she plotted out secret wanderings and gleefully shared the fun of riding a mule-drawn streetcar.

Although the bulge under Kate's big skirts must have brought surprised stares, she managed to absorb the Cajun, Creole, and African-American cultures that gave the city its flavor. A later diary entry recalling her son's birth shows how well she could capture the essence of New Orleans:

> I can remember yet that hot southern day on Magazine street in New Orleans. The noises of the street coming through the open windows; that heaviness with which I dragged myself about; my husband's and mother's solicitude; old Alexandrine the quadroon nurse with her high bandana tignon, her hoop-earrings and placid smile . . .

During the next eight years, Kate had four more sons. Then Oscar's business failed in 1879, and the family had to move to his childhood home. Oscar had grown up on a plantation near the village of Cloutierville (local pronunciation is Cloocherville) on the languid Cane River in northwest Louisiana.

Despite money problems, the first three years there were happy ones. Kate gave birth to their only daughter, and Oscar was "ever jovial and cheerful and fun-loving and really very stout," remembered a friend. He "liked to romp with the children through the house and about the gardens." The same friend recalled that "Kate was devoted to Oscar and thought him perfect."

We do not know Kate's thoughts or feelings during her time in Cloutierville. With a husband and six children, she probably had little time alone for keeping a diary. Still, she found time to create a scandal that the town never forgot.

Cloutierville, Louisiana
· 1879–1884 ·

The Creole men and women of Cloutierville had never seen anyone like twenty-nine-year-old Kate Chopin. Her big-city ways were strange in this sleepy town where a steamboat brought news from the outside world only once a week. The women took notice when she promenaded down the one street in town, twirling her open parasol. They envied her fancy plumed hat and the purple dress with the rose at the throat. And the men's eyes opened wide when she lifted her skirts high enough to show her ankles and calves.

Folks also disapproved of the relaxed way that Kate raised her offspring. She had never forgotten the stifling rules of Sacred Heart Academy and thought that children (and mothers) should enjoy themselves. While Oscar ran the general store two buildings down the street, she rolled cigarettes, practiced imitations of the village priest, and counted her children at the end of the day to make sure no one was missing.

Yet Kate was a careful parent. Lovingly she tucked in her children each night, pulling the mosquito bar, or net, around the metal hoop that hung over each bed. On droopy hot days she swung her new baby in the *branlé*—a round, baby-size hammock that hung on the back porch. Every push of this "quintessence of baby luxury" sent a cooling breeze across little Lelia's plump cheeks. And when one of her sons was sick with fever, she shocked the neighbors by jumping astride her horse and riding it bareback to fetch the doctor. As with everything else in her life, Kate was passionate about motherhood.

Fevers were common in this tropical place, and Oscar's fevers were especially worrisome to Kate. During the fall of 1882, he had recurring bouts of malaria. Eighteen visits from the village doctor throughout October, November, and December were not much help. On the last visit the doctor may have been desperate. He gave Oscar four times the usual amount of quinine, and by December 10, Kate's husband was dead.

This death, above all others she had known, left Kate devastated. But she had to cope with more than grief and six fatherless children. Debtors owed money to the store, and Oscar left her with a string of back taxes to pay. She took over operation of his family lands and worked behind the counter of the store when necessary.

The women of Cloutierville became jealous when their husbands eagerly offered to assist the attractive new widow. Then a handsome but married planter named Albert Sampite began to help Kate with her financial affairs. In Cloutierville, gossip was served up as often as meat pies—at last, here was a way for small-town minds to get even with Kate for her fancy dresses and free-style motherhood. Rumors about the new widow and her married suitor grew as thick as cane breaks on the banks of the river.

Their romance caused such a stir that for years Cloutierville parents raised their children on stories about Kate Chopin and Albert Sampite. According to a playmate of the Chopin children, Kate and Albert were "fond of each other." Albert's grandchildren grew up hearing that he was "infatuated" with her, and Albert's daughter maintained that the affair ruined her parents' marriage. Kate's next-door neighbor always reminded her children that Kate Chopin was a "dirty lady." "You don't know *all* that she did," sniffed the woman.

Did Kate and Albert have a mere flirtation, a brief romance, or a full-blown affair? Cloutierville legend insists that he chased her, but we can never be sure if she let herself be caught. A private person, especially about sex, she would never have revealed such a secret. Perhaps she simply teased

Albert or imagined a wild fling in her mind. Or maybe they did share intimate moments on some languorous Louisiana night. Whatever happened (or did not happen), hints in Kate's later diary entries and the appearance of an Albert-like character in her stories prove that she was obsessed by Albert Sampite.

St. Louis
• 1886–1894 •

*T*wo years after Oscar's death, thirty-three-year-old Kate abruptly packed her belongings and returned to St. Louis with the children. Why did she decide to leave Albert's dark eyes and careless charm? Well known for his vicious temper when drinking, he might have abused her. And she knew they could never marry anyway because the laws of the Catholic Church forbade his divorce. Kate also may have decided not to subject her children to the gossip that circled like gnats around Cloutierville.

Eventually she found a way to forget the wags of the chattering little town. Her doctor in St. Louis had recognized her writing talent from letters she had sent through the years. When he encouraged her to write for publication, she was tempted, since Kate needed the income—at this point in her life, she had more imagination than money.

When Kate began to write, she found someone who had been hiding inside for years—a voice that had grown up with her in the diaries. As in her private writing, this public voice could celebrate the pleasures of music, revel in the joys of reading, or describe the colorful sights and sounds of Louisiana. Most important, it could take her beyond diary writing to the world of forbidden feelings.

Gradually Kate discovered the freedom of fiction. Unable to talk to anyone, even a diary, about her own sensual nature, she could make up characters who admitted theirs. Ten years after leaving Louisiana, she disguised herself and Albert as characters in a diarylike story called "Vagabonds." Just like in a diary, the revealing tale is told in the first person, *I*. The plural title gives a clue to the secret yearning of the narrator (and the author): She loves to tramp alone through the woods and wishes she could wander off into another life.

The story is set in a tiny Cloutierville-like village; the narrator is a Creole woman who runs a general store near the river. When she sells a quart of whiskey to a drunken cousin, they laugh together about the night he tried to kiss another man's wife. As the vignette ends, the woman watches the derelict board a ferry to drift down the river into oblivion. "I could not help thinking that it must be good to prowl sometimes," she wistfully said, "to get close to the black night and lose oneself in its silence and mystery."

The first time Kate penned this sentence, she ended it with "and sin." But like diarists who later censor what they have written, she drew a heavy line through these last two words in the final draft. Kate had always loved the torrid nights of Louisiana—the intoxicating perfumed air, the inky darkness where a woman could have secrets and no one would know.

Perhaps she decided that the story's last words revealed too much about her own dark nights of "sin."

From the beginning of Kate's career, her fiction, like the diary of her debutante years, questioned standards of behavior imposed on women. Her characters and subject matter were unorthodox and might have delayed her literary success. Female characters who broke the mold of the good woman appeared in early stories: One girl chose music over marriage, another was a suffragette.

Kate's first novel, *At Fault,* was the first book about divorce written by an American woman. It proposed the radical idea that marriage was not always in the best interest of a woman. When it was rejected, she paid to have it printed. Fourteen magazines refused her short story about venereal disease before a New Orleans newspaper published it.

Finally, though, Kate's tales of the Cane River region brought her fame. Her first collection of short stories, *Bayou Folk,* was published in 1894. When the book was reviewed in major magazines, it established her national reputation as a writer of local-color literature. Like other regional writers, Kate used details of dress, speech, music, and food to recreate a particular time and place.

Kate based her black, free "mulatto," Cajun, and Creole characters on memories of St. Louis, New Orleans, and Cloutierville. In one of her best-known tales, "Desiree's Baby," she explored the connection between color and gender.

In the story a "mulatto" son is born to a white slaveholding planter and his white wife. To punish her for an assumed infidelity with a black man, the planter casts his wife and their baby out of the house. But truth prevails in one of Kate's famous turnabout endings: The planter, unaware of his own mixed blood, is the real father of the child.

"Desiree's Baby" shows that Kate was quite aware of the consequence of skin color. She was, in truth, part of the racist structure that existed in nineteenth-century America. There had been four enslaved African-Americans in her household when she was five years old. A male slave had held her pony when she rode it as a little girl, and a black woman named Louise may have been Kate's nursemaid.

During the Civil War, both Union and Confederate sympathizers lived in St. Louis. The O'Flahertys supported the Southern cause. When young Kate pulled down a Union flag that someone had hung on the O'Flahertys' porch, her neighbors nicknamed her "The Littlest Rebel." During the Reconstruction years, Oscar Chopin joined the Crescent City White League, a New Orleans version of the Ku Klux Klan.

Kate rarely mentioned African-Americans in her diaries, and black women in her fiction appear as shadowy figures with no names. She identified them only by the labor they provided—a quadroon nurse for the children, a young black girl with the laundry. Despite her upbringing, though, Kate's early local-color stories were sympathetic to African-American women. She portrayed both white and black female characters as devoted mothers, ardent lovers, and casualties of a society in which men held most of the power.

"Father asked us in the eve what fault troubled us most. I said my bad temper."
—Louisa May Alcott

Photo courtesy of the Louisa May Alcott Memorial Association.

"I've felt terribly homesick lately—I know not why, but this longing to see the few dear faces, to hear the kind voices of home is at times almost unbearable."
—Charlotte Forten

Photo courtesy of the Photographs and Prints Division, Schomburg Center for Research in Black Culture, New York Public Library, Astor, Lenox, and Tilden Foundations.

"Ah well I am a strange piece of humanity anyway. Where will I go, and what will I do next?"
—Sarah Jane Foster

Photo courtesy of Wayne Reilly.

"I am invited to a ball and I go. I dance with people I despise, amuse myself with men whose only talent lies in their feet."
—Kate Chopin

Photo by J. A. Scholten. Courtesy of the Missouri Historical Society.

"When I decked mineself up for exhibition purposes,
I looked like a certified check."

—Alice Dunbar-Nelson

"I try not to be rebellious."
—Ida B. Wells-Barnett

Photo courtesy of the
Department of Special Collections,
University of Chicago Library.

"Dance or not to dance?
Charlotte versus mother."
—Charlotte Perkins Gilman

Photo courtesy of the
Schlesinger Library,
Radcliffe College.

St. Louis
• 1894–1896 •

When *Bayou Folk* was published to good reviews in 1894, Kate became a major celebrity in St. Louis. Like her debutante years, the honeymoon trip, and her first months of pregnancy in New Orleans, 1894 brought great changes in her life. Now forty-three years old, she needed to sort out her thoughts during this transitional time. She began a two-year diary she called "Impressions. 1894," and she used it to say privately what she still could not admit in public.

Her impressions of the St. Louis elite had changed little since her teen years. "How immensely uninteresting some 'society' people are!" she exclaimed. "Their refined voices, and refined speech which says nothing—or worse, says something which offends me." Yet she blamed herself for being different. "Why am I so sensitive to manner?" she wondered.

As always, the diary was an agreeable listener. With her "charming" features and abundant hair, friends and family had always called Kate an "Irish beauty." Still, she did not care a bit about growing older or heavier or grayer. "I am younger today at 43 than I was at 23," she wrote. Unlike her friends, she did not worry about the future. "What does it matter," she asked her diary. "I wonder if I shall ever care if it is 43 or 53 or 63. I believe not."

Perhaps because she was older, Kate could at last confess to the diary that she had a sensual nature, though she described it only in vague phrases. "There are a few good things in life—not many, but a few," she confessed. "A soft, firm, magnetic sympathetic hand clasp is one. A walk through the quiet streets at midnight is another." She left this tantalizing clue to a sexual liaison: "And then, there are so many ways of saying good night!"

Another chink in Kate's wall of privacy fell after a visit to her childhood friend, Kitty, who had become a nun. Kitty had given herself "wholly to God," Kate noted in her diary, but she reminded herself that she "had loved—lovers who were not divine." Finally she could refer to her sexuality in her diary—a step toward admitting that she still had exciting memories of Albert Sampite. And five years later she immortalized him in her masterpiece, *The Awakening*.

The Awakening
· *1899* ·

*K*ate re-created her former suitor as Alcée Arobin, the dashing flirt of *The Awakening*. Like Albert, Alcée is dangerous. A well-known ladies' man, he has affairs with married women, including Edna Pontellier, the main character of the book.

Just as Kate did not mention her own sexuality in her diaries until 1894, the fictional Edna has long denied the boredom of her marriage. For years she has lived "unthinkingly, as we walk, move, sit, stand, go through the daily treadmill of the life which has been portioned out to us." While vacationing on an island off the Gulf Coast, she has servants to care for the children and the house. With little to do but swim, sketch, and receive visitors, though, her life seems meaningless.

Edna begins to rebel against the tedium of her days. She stays awake all night outside the house, even after her husband commands her to come to bed. She listens to piano music, yearning to hear her own passion released in the wild tumble of notes. When music cannot satisfy her, she desperately tries to express her feelings through art.

Edna's wave of defiance gathers strength as she moves out of her husband's house, its iron-barred windows a symbol of her stagnant life. Despite an infatuation with one man and a hollow affair with Alcée Arobin, Edna despairs. She is sure that she will never escape her destiny. Finally Edna chooses the only lover she thinks can ever understand: the great emptiness of the sea. Despondent, she walks "on and on" into the warm waters of the gulf, seduced by its "whispering" voice and "sensuous" touch.

Within the pages of *The Awakening,* Kate Chopin posed questions she could never ask in her diary. Wondering how a mother could be someone besides a parent, she created a character to wrestle with the same problem. And through the fictional character of Edna, Kate struggled to reconcile her own sensual nature with the traditional image of a woman. Having known temptation herself, she imagined what a woman would find if she pursued illicit love.

The novel also let Kate express mixed feelings about marriage. She did not oppose wedlock, for apparently she had a satisfactory marriage—she told her 1894 diary that if Oscar came back to life, she would give up "every thing that has come into my life since." She admitted, though, she would have to pay a price to make that wish come true. "To do that," she wrote in her diary, "I would have to forget the past ten years of my growth—my real growth."

As society defined marriage in the nineteenth century, there was little room for a wife's fulfillment outside the home. Intelligent, creative women like Kate often found themselves incapable of change, as stifled by the restrictions of matrimony and motherhood as they were by corsets and stays. Through Edna, Kate defined the dilemma of the ideal woman, then created a dramatic, though tragic solution to it.

And she found a way to keep romantic memories of Albert Sampite alive. If Kate's 1894 diary prepared her to create Alcée in *The Awakening,* that novel may have awakened Kate's experimentation with erotica in "The Storm." Kate wrote this daring story while waiting for *The Awakening* to be published. Knowing that a woman would be censored for writing about adultery between a racially mixed couple, she never submitted it to an editor. For the nineteenth century, the writing was quite suggestive: "He pushed her hair back from her face that was warm and steaming. Her lips were as red and moist as pomegranate seed. Her white neck and a glimpse of her full, firm bosom disturbed him powerfully."

Kate could have predicted that no editor would publish "The Storm." But she had no idea that literary critics would snub *The Awakening* like a socially incorrect visitor in a St.

Louis salon. When the book was published in 1899, a St. Louis newspaper headline described it as "The Story of a Lady Most Foolish." Another paper declared that it was "not a healthy book." A Boston paper said that Edna should have "flirted less and cared more for others."

Edna had broken all the rules, and so had Kate. A nineteenth-century woman writer was expected to create a moral atmosphere for her readers, not write a story about an unfaithful wife and dissatisfied mother. There were a few favorable reviews, and Kate's friends called her an "artist" and a "genius." But the negative reactions sickened, even cowed her. She had what she described as "a severe spell of illness." And the following year she submitted a story to an editor with the apology, "I can't imagine that you will care for this little sketch."

In a final weak protest against behavior codes for women, the mutinous voice of her early diaries found its way into print. A few months after *The Awakening* was published, she wrote an article about herself for a St. Louis paper. "Suppose I do smoke cigarettes?" she asked defiantly. "Suppose I don't smoke cigarettes." Other than a few children's tales and some stories on safe topics, though, she wrote little else after 1899.

On a warm Saturday in August 1904, Kate set out for one of her solitary walks. The World's Fair had opened in St. Louis that year, and the edge of the enormous fairground was just six blocks from her home. She was one of the first to buy a season ticket. Almost every day she slipped away to enjoy the colorfully lit waterfalls, Scott Joplin's ragtime piano music, and the military parades.

But this was one of the hottest days of the summer. Kate walked more than usual and came home tired. Around midnight she felt a sharp pain in her head. A few moments after calling for her son, she was unconscious, and in two days she was dead, probably of a stroke.

Kate Chopin never carried a protest sign or wrote articles for women's rights. There is no evidence that she even had any personal interest in the suffrage movement. She left the risks of daring marches and political publications to activists like Ida B. Wells and Charlotte Perkins Gilman.

Yet tentatively in her diaries, then clearly in her stories, she observed how society's expectations could destroy a woman's spirit. There were few people with whom she could share these radical ideas about women's freedom. "Naturally reserved," she kept her thoughts to herself until diary writing and story writing let her liberate them. Then, while other women were writing wholesome stories that could be read around the family circle, Kate Chopin used fiction to tell her deepest secrets about marriage, motherhood, romance, and sex.

ALICE DUNBAR-NELSON

· · · · ·

"Genteel Poet"

❦

New Orleans
· 1875–1898 ·

Alice Ruth Moore was born on a steamy July day in New Orleans, Louisiana, in 1875. That summer, in the same city, Kate Chopin was expecting another son. It is unlikely that their families ever met, though. Kate and Alice shared the sultry skies of New Orleans, but they lived in separate worlds of black and white.

Because Alice was a light-skinned African-American, she was caught midway between these worlds, first while growing up, then as a writer. Alice considered herself black, but she appeared white. Though she looked white, she was mistreated as a black. Yet blacks taunted her because she could pass as *au fait*.

The first African-American woman to publish a book of short fiction, her stories are set in New Orleans and peopled with Creoles of color. But the author studiously avoided mention of race. Though her early writing reflects racial uncertainty, Alice finally discovered who she was and what she really wanted to say—after years of keeping a diary.

It is no wonder Alice was unsure of her identity, for she grew up in the most color-conscious city in the country. White New Orleanians had always grouped themselves by culture—French Creole, Spanish Creole, and Cajun. And they divided African-Americans by color—black, mulatto, quadroon, octoroon, and mixed Indian.

With their status defined by skin color, light-skinned free African-Americans enjoyed an aristocratic position when compared with their enslaved "darker brethren," as Alice once called them. After the Civil War, they perpetuated the color caste system and continued to live in separate neighborhoods. They thought of themselves as superior to newly freed blacks, who coveted the elite's higher status even as they scorned it.

Consequently Alice Ruth Moore kept secrets about her ancestry long before she kept a diary. Almost no one knew that her mother, Patricia, had been a slave in Opelousas, Louisiana. And for years even Alice was unaware that the man who had held her mother in slavery withheld news of the Emancipation Proclamation from his slaves.

Instead he took them to Texas, where Union troops finally forced him to let them go after two years. Alice recalled her mother's description: "Inflexible Yankee soldiers on each side of the white-haired old man, his sobbing daughters and wife, the open-mouthed indignant and unforgiving slaves, for most of them were of mixed Indian blood."

Patricia and the other freed slaves left their former slaveholder and his promises of new cabins and back wages. They swam across two rivers and walked for three months to get back to Louisiana. At some point Patricia moved one hundred and thirty-five miles east to New Orleans and became a dressmaker, one of the few skilled occupations available to African-American women after the Civil War.

Secrets about parents may be the hardest to admit, even to a diary. Alice wrote of her mother's enslavement only once—in a letter. She never told her diaries about her father, either. We know only that he was a seaman named Joseph who might have been white and who might not have been married to her mother.

Alice's mother desperately wanted to forget her enslavement and to seek the social standing of lighter-skinned blacks. The family was poor, but Patricia managed to put Alice and her older sister, Lelia, through six years of public schools in New Orleans. She made "print frocks" for them to wear, kept their clothes "carefully washed," and scrimped to buy them pretty hair ribbons.

Alice was a "timid, scared, rabbit sort of child," but she quickly learned to defend herself in a "monster" public school of twenty-five-hundred children. The darker children tormented her. They called her a "half white nigger," ripped the ribbons out of her hair, and dipped her curls into the inkwell. In the seventh grade Alice transferred to a private black school for the children of "aristocrats." Because she had fair skin, it was easy for her to blend in with people she called the "mulatto" elite, "descendants of free antebellum Negroes."

Patricia was proud when seventeen-year-old Alice graduated from a two-year teacher-training program in 1892. With two educated children, she now had achieved a middle-class status and put the degradation of slavery behind her. The lovely Alice became noted for her "cultured and refined manners" and was considered a lady of "much grace" and "superior intellect." And for all anyone knew, Patricia Moore and her family had *always* been aristocrats.

Young Alice Moore learned how to be cool and calm in public. By the age of nineteen, she was already employed as a schoolteacher and the only black secretary in New Orleans. In private, however, she was as unpredictable as a tropical storm—moody, impulsive, and baffled by her treatment as a light-skinned black.

During her first year in high school, she struggled with heartbreak when a "boy of deep darkness" rejected her. "I loved Eddie," remembered Alice later, but he told her he would rather walk alone than "demean himself by walking with a mere golden butterfly." Then, as a beginning "fair" teacher, Alice endured veiled insults in "hot shamed silence" from her darker-skinned colleagues.

She might have recorded some of these turbulent feelings in a diary. No journal survives from Alice's girlhood days, but she left a clue that she might have kept one. When she was twenty-four, she created an autobiographical character who recalled New Orleans and the "old diary-keeping" days. "I shan't keep a diary any more now," the Alice-like person vowed. "It shall be like those that I used to burn years ago."

Keeping a diary was unusual for a young black woman in the nineteenth century. A typical middle-class white girl received her first diary as a gift from relatives. Struggling middle-class black parents, however, might have thought diaries were an unnecessary expense and a frivolous waste of time. As Alice's fictional character said, "I sit idly dreaming with the diary for an excuse." Besides, the road to a better life was hard and full of grief. Why live through it a second time on paper?

Alice's family remembered her as the gifted one, the "genius." Words came easily to the young girl. Searching for a comfortable writing style, she tried on different literary forms as easily as dresses. During her teen years she experimented with poems, stories, essays, and reviews. One of her story sketches was published before she was twenty, and in 1895 she paid to have a collection of short stories and poetry printed: *Violets and Other Tales.*

Like Kate Chopin, Alice based her stories on the Creole culture of her native New Orleans. Perhaps because she felt so unsettled about her color, she disguised African-American characters behind vague phrases like "dusky-eyed" and "dat light gal." Mirroring the popular reading tastes of the time, these local-color sketches are romantic melodramas that reflect the manners and customs of Creole society.

One day in 1895, Alice received a letter from a man she had never met. Paul Laurence Dunbar, the first professional African-American poet (he penned the line "I know why the caged bird sings"), had read Alice's sketch in a Boston magazine. Her talent impressed him. He may also have been taken by her delicate beauty, since Alice's picture accompanied the story.

"Pardon my boldness in addressing you," his letter began. "I should like to exchange opinions and work with you if you will agree." Paul enclosed one of his own poems as proof of his "credentials, with as little egotism as possible." Alice wrote back, and their letters quickly changed from formal to personal. "Let us not be literary in our letters, let us be friendly. I like it better, don't you?" asked Paul. Thus began their two-year courtship through the mail.

In the middle of the blossoming romance, Alice and her

entire family—mother, sister, and sister's husband—left New Orleans in 1896. Alice moved east to Massachusetts with them, then went alone to Brooklyn, New York, to teach school. Throughout the moves she and Paul continued to write, falling in love by letter before they saw each other in person. When they finally met one cold evening in 1897, Paul gave Alice his mother's wedding ring, and they became engaged on the same night.

Alice's family did not approve of Paul. In many ways he reminded them of the painful past they wanted to forget. Not only did he write "dialect" poetry in black English, he composed songs for the "coon" minstrel shows so popular at the turn of the century.

Like Patricia Moore, Paul's mother had sacrificed to secure an education for her son. But Alice's family was ashamed of Matilda Dunbar because she was a former slave and unskilled laundress. Worst of all, Paul Laurence Dunbar had dark skin. Although he was handsome, they sensed that the illusion of aristocracy would be hard to maintain if Alice married a man as "black as sin."

Early in 1898, Alice begged Paul to marry her. She might have thought she was pregnant. "Have pity on my weakness for the dear God's sake," she wrote, "and make me yours *legally*." The couple had a secret wedding, announced their marriage, then moved to Washington, D.C.

Washington, D.C.
• 1898–1902 •

The next four years were troubled, even violent ones for Alice. No diary from this period exists, but she accidentally devised a diarylike outlet for her confused feelings. Sometime around 1899, twenty-four-year-old Alice began a novel in the form of a diary: *Confessions of a Lazy Woman*. As in a real diary, the manuscript features dated entries, outspoken criticisms of friends and family, and revelations about the author's personality. Alice did not realize it, but the Lazy Woman of the title is Alice in disguise.

Completely different in tone from her earlier fiction, the novel allowed Alice to experiment with her "I" voice—one that was down-to-earth, witty, and often "unladylike" in style. Twenty-two years later, in 1921, she would release a similar voice in a real diary. And in 1926, she would begin a series of peppery newspaper columns. The same forthright, humorous Alice can be heard in all three of these first-person genres.

Read as a novel, *Confessions* is a pointless work. Alice's literary agent labeled it "monotonous," and even Alice called it "senseless drivel." She told Paul she supposed she was writing it for "amusement," but why did she waste her time on one hundred pages of worthless manuscript? Keeping a real diary would have been as extravagant as silk. But a novel

written as a diary could provide temporary escape for a
young woman caught in an ill-fated marriage.

Read as a diary, *Confessions* is a vault of hidden details
about Alice's marriage to Paul Laurence Dunbar. Although
they supported each other's writing careers, the rest of
the world forgot that Alice was already a published author.
After Alice Moore became Mrs. Dunbar, she was known
mainly as her husband's "helpmeet" who took dictation and
typed his writings. She even lost her name. When she wrote a
volume of local-color stories to accompany a volume of
Paul's poetry, a newspaper called her "Paul Dunbar's gifted
wife."

This passage from *Confessions* reveals Alice's inner tur-
moil about her marriage. The Matron of the Sea is a fairy
godmother figure for the Lazy Woman who keeps the diary:

> "My dear," she [Matron of the Sea] asked breath-
> lessly as soon as she had kissed one of my cheeks
> turned [to] her, "Where have you been? I haven't
> seen you since you married. Fie, to bury yourself
> just because you have a husband. You mustn't do it
> dear, you must not. It's poor policy. I will not allow
> you to make the mistake of so many young married
> women. Now haven't you been dreadfully lonely in
> the last year or two?"

Then the Matron urges the Lazy Woman to join women's
clubs. The diarist wonders if her husband would approve.
The Matron sternly replies:

> Some men like to have their wives merge their identities in them and never realize that a woman might object. There are women of course— "words cannot describe the severity of the Matron's tone and manner,"—who countenance and even submit to that sort of thing. I am happy to say that I do not number such women among my friends.

Alice's own shaky sense of self is apparent in the diarist's cheerful reply to the Matron: "But I never had any identity to merge!" Had Alice buried herself "just because" she had a husband? Was she "dreadfully lonely"? We know she became active in black women's clubs during this time, perhaps out of the need for a life apart from Paul. Marriage to the famous poet had left her, like the woman in the diary/novel, secretly unfulfilled beneath an "iron mask of reserve."

Like any diary, *Confessions of a Lazy Woman* is rambling and without plot. Characters are casually mentioned, then disappear without explanation. Still, it is easy to recognize Alice's spouse.

Alice based the Lazy Woman's husband, Ned, on her own husband, Paul. Like Paul, whom she remembered as "delightful beyond compare" when sober, Ned "is a very sensible man and a very fitting companion for his wife." But sometimes Ned makes them both miserable.

In a tone that teeters on the edge of sarcasm, Ned and the Lazy Woman snap at each other throughout the manuscript. A litany of "Ned says" reveals Paul Dunbar's personality and

Alice's troubles with him: "Ned says they [women's clubs] are noisy and wrangling in their meetings"; "Ned says that he hears there are women who have to be beaten"; "Ned will not allow anyone to abuse me but himself."

During the time that Alice wrote *Confessions,* Paul began to drink heavily. Bourbon soothed the coughing attacks caused by his tuberculosis and gave him courage for his public poetry recitals. As Paul developed a dependency on alcohol and on the heroin tablets prescribed by his doctor, the couple's arguments became more frequent and abusive. But who could Alice tell except her diary/novel?

Alice was understandably ambivalent about children when she wrote *Confessions.* During this time she and Paul were trying to conceive a child. While he was away on a trip, she wrote to him that she was making almost daily visits to a woman doctor "to be tortured" for fertility "treatments." The doctor appears in *Confessions* as a female "Little Doctor."

Alice's mixed feelings about children are apparent in the Lazy Woman's humorous description of the "Elf-Child." The daughter of a visiting friend, the Elf-Child is a "little beast." She is the "Original Omnivorous One" who sneaks biscuits off the plate and gorges herself on potatoes.

The novel's surprise ending uncovers Alice's private fantasy. "Last week they laid something in my arms," Alice as Lazy Woman wrote. "It was pink and soft and helpless." Then the reader learns that the confessions of a lazy woman were actually the confessions of a pregnant woman. The diarist expects to be quite busy, and she ends with, "I must help my Best Beloved [husband] admire baby."

When Alice wrote these lines, she must have longed for a child. Perhaps she thought that a baby would save her sinking marriage. There would be no children, however. In 1902, after "four bitter years" of marriage, Paul came home after a drinking bout. Alice remembered he was in a "beastly condition." He behaved "disgracefully," then beat her.

Worse, he went to a bar and told lies about her. After a trip to New York where he spread a "vile story," she forced him to leave the house. The pair divorced, and they never saw each other again before Paul died of tuberculosis four years later in 1906.

Alice as the Lazy Woman spoke for all diarists when she defined a diary in the first entry of *Confessions*:

> If kept in the right spirit, it means a record of things both seen and unseen, all recorded in a strictly conscientious fashion. It means, too, that one must crystallize one's secret thoughts and longings and desires into written words, thereby giving speech to hitherto inarticulate voices.

Still, as the Lazy Woman noted, a diary could be dangerous, too.

> For if evil thoughts come to one and are quickly dismissed as unworthy, they are gone and the only memory of them is as a disagreeable wind from an arid plain, while if put on paper, they are always there to stare one boldly in the face.

Confessions of a Lazy Woman was never published, but it served its purpose. When Alice wrote the novel, she was too young and in love to stare "boldly in the face" at her childlessness, an alcoholic husband, and a lost professional identity. Like Kate Chopin, who imagined an affair through *The Awakening,* Alice invented another life through a diary. By writing *Confessions of a Lazy Woman,* she could make her problems briefly disappear and her fantasies come true.

Wilmington
· *1902–1926* ·

*T*wenty-seven-year-old Alice and her sister urgently needed jobs when they moved to Wilmington, Delaware, in 1902. After having four children, Lelia and her husband had also separated. Together the two sisters needed to support themselves, their mother, and Lelia's son and three daughters.

Both women found teaching positions at Howard High School in Wilmington. Alice taught there for the next eighteen years. Students loved her "outgoing personality and charm," and fellow teachers respected her "high sense of honor, integrity, and independence." Perhaps it was Alice's independence that prompted her to make a mistake she kept secret for years.

Few people ever knew that Alice married a fellow teacher at Howard High School in 1910. Twenty-two-year-old Arthur

Callis was twelve years younger than Alice. He called their four-year romance "the jewel around which his whole life was built." Yet Alice remembered their wedding day as the time she and Arthur "made fools of ourselves at Old Swedes Church."

Despite Arthur's "great passion," Alice ended the marriage within a few months. And in 1916, forty-one-year-old Alice married for the last time. Now she was Mrs. Alice Dunbar-Nelson. Robert Nelson, or Bobbo (pronounced Bob-O), was a steady, dependable partner. She later told her diary that he was "first, last and always, the best of all."

Within the next two years, though, fickle Alice became involved with another man. Their infatuation began when they met during World War I in Washington. A temporary wartime flirtation, it may have been consummated only by an exchange of rings and a few love poems. Alice wrote these on loose-leaf paper that she called her "Dream Book."

Until 1921, Alice confined her true writing voice to private manuscripts like *Confessions of a Lazy Woman* and the "Dream Book." Then she suffered a great loss when her adored niece, Lelia, died in January 1921. She kept her grief inside for six months but finally unmasked her feelings in a five-by-seven-inch brown notebook.

Like an adult talking to a child, she began by giving herself a lecture: "Had I enough sense to keep a diary all these years . . . there would be less confusion in my mind about lots of things." Then she firmly explained the purpose of the diary to herself: "Now I begin this day to keep the record that should have been kept long since."

Alice's diary writing was far livelier than any of her short stories. From 1920 to 1922, she and Bobbo published a political newspaper called *The Advocate*. Her diary entries for these years are written in a tense, white-knuckle style, full of cliffhanger tales about borrowing money and meeting deadlines. When the newspaper folded, Alice's crisp comment was more convincing than any dialogue in her short stories: "No money, no *Advocate*. SO!"

During the 1920s, as Alice faithfully recorded her feelings in a page-per-day memorandum book, she developed a confident political voice. Popular on the lecture circuit, she campaigned for women's suffrage, visited President Harding at the White House to discuss racial concerns, and headed the Anti-Lynching Crusaders in Delaware. She did not forget her literary ambitions. Now forty-six, she abandoned short stories but continued to write poetry.

Alice was a frequent contributor to the prestigious black magazine *Opportunity*. Along with other magazines in Harlem, New York, *Opportunity* published many of the poems, short stories, and essays written during the renaissance of black literature and art of the twenties. In 1926, when she was fifty-one, one of Alice's poems won honorable mention in the magazine's annual literary competition.

She almost missed the awards dinner in Harlem. Luckily her niece Pauline yanked her "out of bed early," and her sister, Lelia, lent her ten dollars to travel to New York. Alice told her diary she had arrived so late that she was afraid to go into the dining room. But the literary lights of the evening— James Weldon Johnson, Countee Cullen, Carl Van Vechten—gave her a warm welcome. "Moving from table to table," Alice fit in easily with the other guests, who recognized her as a writer and the former wife of the well-known poet.

Although Alice's romantic poetry and formless short stories do not appeal to modern tastes, she was a respected member of the Harlem Renaissance. Known as one of the "Genteel Poets," her writing links nineteenth-century Romantic literature to the more racially conscious books of the twenties by Nella Larsen, Jessie Fauset, and Zora Neale Hurston.

Alice might have created more memorable literature if an early story about skin color had been published. While married to Paul, twenty-five-year-old Alice had written a short story called "Stones of the Village." She based it on her experiences in the "monster" school of her childhood. The main character was a boy, but the feelings of shame belonged to Alice.

The boy of the story, Victor, is a light-skinned child from New Orleans. His grandmother refuses to allow him to play with the darker children. They retaliate by calling him a "white nigger." When Victor is able, he abandons his race and passes for white. After growing up, he marries a white woman, has a family, and prospers in business. But Victor is driven mad with guilt for ignoring his black heritage. In a cautionary ending, he punishes himself by taking his own life.

Alice sent "Stones of the Village" to a magazine editor and suggested that she could expand it into a novel. But he refused, believing that Americans would "dislike" reading about the "color-line." If he had accepted it, Alice would have made literary history in 1900 as the first African-American woman to publish a story on the sensitive subject of "passing." Instead, rejection muffled the young writer's voice.

Americans did not want to read about the "color-line," but Alice had to live with it every day. Perhaps the worst part for her was being "too white" to get a job intended for blacks. And if she tried to pass for white to get a much-needed position, black employees reported her. In public, Alice stood united with the "Mother-race." In private, though, the "wishy-washy sentimentalism about persecuted black ones of the race" disgusted her.

If Alice was a victim of black racism, she was also guilty of keeping it alive. She larded her diary with derogatory references to darker African-Americans, calling a West Indian a "monkey chaser." An acquaintance didn't go to a birthday party, Alice wrote, because she would have looked like a "fly in a flour barrel" in a group of "blondes and high browns."

Reading Alice's diary, it becomes easier to understand her preoccupation with color. Once Alice took her nieces to the theater. She had prepurchased the tickets, but then panicked as she approached the entrance. What if the ticket taker refused them all entrance when he saw her darker relatives? "I choked with apprehension," she remembered in her diary, "realized that I was invoking trouble and must not think destructive things, and went on in. Nothing happened. How splendid it must be never to have any apprehension about one's treatment any where."

Alice's description of her dread is wrenching to read. That

depth of feeling seldom showed in her fiction and poetry, however. Too soon in her career, Alice learned that mixing literature with the raw reality of black life was not a recipe for a woman writer's success, and she never addressed race in her fiction again. Instead, she stifled her clearest voice and tried to "produce literature," a term she used often in her diary. She mocked her own efforts when she enclosed the words in quotation marks, and like her published stories and poems, the phrase has an artificial ring.

Wilmington
· 1926 ·

Five years of diary writing finally liberated Alice's tart, sassy voice. In 1926 she began a weekly newspaper column called "From a Woman's Point of View." At last, the amusing phrases so natural to her diary writing ("we felt floppy" and "she came in like Death eating a cracker") were available to the reading public. Now every Saturday she could express her opinions, complain, joke, and needle both blacks and whites.

As a book and movie critic, she kept track of black culture as portrayed by whites. When the white author Carl Van Vechten included a middle-class African-American woman in his novel *Nigger Heaven*, Alice praised his "plain acceptance of a cultivated brown woman." But she pointed out the absurdity of choosing white actors for films about blacks. "It does seem unfortunate, does it not," she asked sardonically, "that there is no little colored girl to do the part of Topsy in the forthcoming film of UNCLE TOM'S CABIN?"

Alice's sarcasm could cut like a machete through sugar-cane. "The microphone records and transmits the victim's dying moans," she reported about a lynching being broadcast over the radio. "Floridians far and near, who are unable to be among those present, tune in on Station S-A-V-A-G-E and have their cup of cruelty filled to its poisoned brim."

She did not spare the knife for her fellow African-Americans. Capital letters howl her contempt for blacks who were supposed to be working against the segregation of train cars:

> The North Carolina Inter-Racial Committee has appointed a committee to investigate traveling conditions in the Jim Crow cars, and to insist upon better Jim Crow cars. TO INSIST UPON BETTER JIM CROW CARS! Can you beat it?

And she wasted no time addressing what it meant to be a woman. Her very first column noted that "Black and brown and yellow and white" women are "the backbone of the world." Women are the dependable ones, she said, who hold the "jazz-mad, radio-crazed hysteric nation" together.

On the subject of women's work, Alice's public writing mirrored the thoughts in her diary. She complained to her diary that "Bob-O is perfectly sure it is a sin to wash necessary clothes on Sunday but not a sin to type-write, write newspaper articles, go on excursions, cook huge dinners, commit adultery [make love to Bob-O]."

Using similar language, she announced in her column that black men did not want women to get the vote. They were afraid that the women would have "no time for washing, ironing, cooking, scrubbing, sewing, baking, wiping the children's noses or getting them ready for Sunday school." In her diary and in her column, Alice Dunbar-Nelson recognized that there was more than one way to keep a woman enslaved.

Wilmington
· *1930–1935* ·

*W*ith the diary applauding from the sideline, Alice continued her spirited newspaper columns midway into 1930. The freedom of journalistic writing may have unlocked her most deeply buried thoughts—that year, Alice revealed her greatest secret to the diary: her sexual relationships with women. A backward look through all of her diaries reveals a trail of clues pointing to a growing affection for women. Like a long cycle of courtship, her lesbianism evolved from physical attraction to subtle romance to sexual involvement and emotional commitment.

The first clue is a poem Alice wrote in her "Dream Book" in 1921 about Inez—a woman with "dusk eyes" who stirred "the depths of passionate desire!" By 1930 she was completely open about *"A Perfect"* day she spent in San Francisco with a woman named Fay. With "Emotions of beauty too profound to describe," Alice called it "a day ever to be remembered." The perfect day ended with Fay spending the night. Open in her diary with the names of women, she was discreet about the details. She underlined coded words to refer to sex—once she and a friend, Helene, had an "early morning *talk*" that left Helene "walking on air."

Alice led a dual life as wife to Bobbo and lover to women friends. Yet she felt little conflict about her sexuality, perhaps because she and Bobbo were more like close associates than spouses. They lent each other money, shared the other's trials and triumphs, and freely gave encouragement and comfort. Their marriage worked well as they defined it for themselves. Sex may have been a component at first, but if that changed along the way to warm companionship, it did not alter the strength of their bond.

In 1931 Alice abandoned the diary, possibly because of health problems. She had high blood pressure, an early sign of her later heart disease. Constant worry from living on the edge of poverty surely complicated her hypertension. As the Depression worsened, money was especially scarce. "Fear, fear, fear—," Alice panicked in her diary, "it haunts me, pursues, dries my mouth, parches my lips and shakes my knees, nauseates me. Fear! And no money—yet."

At one point the anxiety was so great that she could no longer turn to her diary for solace. "I could not write before when the misery and wretchedness and disappointment and worry were so close to me that to write it out was impossible, and not to write it out, foolish."

Despite the troubles, irrepressible Alice still enjoyed life. During 1931 she had her hair bobbed, saw a constant stream of plays, and took great pleasure in eating good meals when they were available. Always a curious person, the sight of an automated milk factory milking five hundred cows at one time thrilled her enough to record the event in her diary. And life was "glorious" when she spent an evening sipping brandy with her women friends.

The existing diaries of Alice Dunbar-Nelson end in 1931. A year later Bobbo found a secure job in Philadelphia, and she spent the last years of her life free from severe financial worries. In 1935, at the age of sixty, Alice died of chronic heart disease at the University of Pennsylvania Hospital. Bobbo brought Alice's body back to Wilmington to be cremated. Then he scattered her ashes over the Delaware River, following his wife's wishes to have her remains strewn to "the four winds, either over land or sea."

For Alice, keeping a diary was a blessing and a burden. Once when she fell behind in her entries, she called the notebook "a weight on my heart." Thinking the diary "would be important one day," she felt it was her duty to record her life. But her diaries are much more than daily logs. They reveal how complicated life could be for African-American women in the first third of the twentieth century.

Alice's actual diaries—four different notebooks totaling two thousand pages—are an interesting mess of cards, invitations, clippings, and loose pages. As multilayered as her personality, the notebooks are a visual metaphor for a diarist who had to be many people at once: daughter, sister, aunt, wife, lover, teacher, writer, lecturer, and political activist. For a woman whose color, gender, and sexual choices forced her to keep an assortment of secrets, the diaries also gave her a way to speak until she found a voice of her own.

IDA B. WELLS

. . . . .

"Brilliant Iola"

Holly Springs, Mississippi
· 1862–1878 ·

Sometimes Ida B. Wells felt like an oddity. "I am an anomaly to myself as well as to others," she complained to her diary at twenty-three. "I do not wish to be married but I do wish for the society of the gentlemen." But there was nothing wrong with Ida. She was independent, outspoken, and able to make her own decisions—qualities considered "masculine" in her day, yet ones that fit her as snugly as a straw hat. Exchanging rings at the altar would be easy, she knew. But she was not willing to trade the strong side of herself for wifely compliance. She simply had too much work to do.

Ida's pride and independence often offended people who expected to see the softer side of her personality. These same traits, however, helped transform a tragic youth into a courageous life. At the age of twenty-two, she became a fighter for women's and black civil rights. By the time she was thirty, she was the feisty leader of the anti-lynching crusade. And for the rest of her life, Ida, like a character in a book that she admired in her diary, was "sometimes man, sometimes woman" as she bravely confronted the battles of the early civil rights movement.

She was born into slavery in Holly Springs, Mississippi, on July 16, 1862. Both of her parents had been enslaved too, and after they were all freed by the Emancipation Proclamation in 1863, Jim and Lizzie Wells celebrated by getting married again as free people.

Lizzie, a renowned cook, raised the eight Wells children. She marched the "whole brood" to Sunday school every week, made them finish their homework, and trained them to do household tasks. During slavery Jim Wells had been apprenticed to a white builder. When he was freed, he earned enough as an independent carpenter to buy a house for his large family.

Ida remembered in her diary that she led a "butterfly existence" when she was growing up. She flitted from school-work to household duties to playtime during her sheltered childhood years. But her most important job, she recalled, was to go to school and learn all she could.

Before the Civil War, Ida's mother had survived beatings by slave traders and slaveholders. After the war, Jim Wells weathered the violent threats of the Ku Klux Klan. But neither of her parents was strong enough to fight the "Scourge of the South" that spread through the Mississippi Valley soon after Ida turned sixteen. She remembered this as the end of her time as a "happy, light-hearted school girl" and the beginning of her "darkest days."

The calamity arrived late in the summer of 1878, while Ida was visiting her grandmother in nearby Tippah County, Mississippi. One day, three horsemen called to her from the gate of the house. She recognized them as her parents' friends and neighbors. When she eagerly asked them to come in and tell her all the news from home, they produced a letter from a doctor in Holly Springs.

The words seemed to jump off the page—the worst epidemic of yellow fever in the nation's history had spread to her little hometown. "Jim and Lizzie Wells have both died of the fever," the message read. "They died within twenty-four hours of each other. . . . Send word to Ida."

The farmhouse immediately became a "house of mourning," Ida remembered. Torn by grief and worry, she demanded to leave right away. She knew her six younger brothers and sisters needed her. One sister was confined to a wheelchair, and her baby brother, Stanley, was only nine months old (another brother had died years before).

But her grandmother refused to let her go. Better that she should stay until the worst of the epidemic had passed, her grandmother insisted, than to risk the horrible fate of many fever victims: chills, fever, yellowed skin, black vomit, and death. Impatiently Ida Bell agreed to wait a few days—one of the few times in her life when she gave in during an argument.

Three days later, she arrived in Holly Springs on a caboose draped with black. Out of 120,000 cases of fever, 20,000 people had died. There weren't enough riders for a passenger train, and even this freight train had lost two conductors to the "yellow jack." When Ida reached home, she discovered that the baby had already died. Most of her remaining sisters and brothers were in bed with mild cases of the fever, but they soon recovered.

James Wells had been a member of the Masons, and now his Masonic brothers became guardians of the Wells children. The men gathered at the house on a Sunday afternoon to discuss the fate of the orphans. Ida sat silently as she listened to them divide her family like a basket of apples. Her two brothers would be apprenticed to carpenters. Two sisters would be given away to families who wanted girls. But her paralyzed sister, Genie, would have to go to the poorhouse, since no one wanted a child in a wheelchair. And Ida, the oldest, could take care of herself.

Ida was a bit spoiled and used to being noticed. When no one had asked her opinion on the matter, she wanted to stamp her foot. Why, her mother and father would turn over in their graves if they knew the children were to be split apart! The Wells family owned the house, she hotly announced, and they would continue to live there—together!

At first the men laughed at her. How would a sixteen-year-old "butterfly" schoolgirl raise a family alone? they asked. But Ida could sound like she had her hands on her hips and her chin up in the air, even when she didn't. When the Masons heard the angry tone in her voice, they let her have her way. As she later remembered in her diary, she was a "hard headed" girl capable of "childish rage and jealousy."

There must have been times, though, when Ida regretted her decision. The next year was terribly hard. Now she was father and mother to five brothers and sisters. She barely had time to mourn her parents' deaths or the sudden end of her own childhood, and the experience hardened her into an angry young woman.

The Freedmen's Aid Society had started a school for African-Americans in Holly Springs after the Civil War. All grades were taught there, including the college level. Ida (along with her mother, who learned to read the Bible) was among the first students—she later recalled that she read every novel in the school.

But she was forced to leave the school that eventually became Rust College. Ida maintained in her published autobiography that the Masons advised her to quit and find a job, though this contradicts her diary entries. Easily qualified to teach in a country school six miles away, sweet-faced Ida removed her big hair bow and pinned her hair up into a bun. Still a girl on the inside, she lengthened her dresses to make her pupils think she was a grown woman.

Every Sunday she left the children with their grandmother, climbed on the back of a poky white mule, and rode out to the country. She boarded with a different family each week, earning a "munificent" twenty-five dollars per month. The weeks were long and lonely, but compared with weekends, they must have seemed like holidays.

Each Friday afternoon Ida rode back to town, carrying a load of country butter and eggs for her family to eat. On Saturdays she started a grinding round of chores: cooking, washing, ironing. She might have acted like a grown-up, but adult responsibility sat as heavily as a fieldstone on her narrow shoulders. Raising her brothers and sisters was so difficult that she was certain she would want no children of her own.

Memphis, Tennessee
· *1879–1885* ·

*I*da was relieved when her aunts came to the rescue one year after the epidemic. Her mother's sister offered to care for the two boys and Genie. When an aunt in nearby Memphis, Tennessee, took the youngest girls, Ida left Holly Springs with them. She found a teaching job near Memphis, riding the train to and from school every day. Life was a little easier for the next few years, although she still missed her carefree school days. Then an incident in the spring of 1884 thrust her into the public arena, where she remained for the rest of her life.

On the afternoon of May 4, twenty-two-year-old Ida boarded the train as usual and took a seat in the ladies' car. The conductor, however, refused to take her ticket, insisting that she move to the smokers' car. This car, Ida recalled, was "already filled with colored people and those who were smoking." In the 1880s, railroad smoking cars were sickening places. The dirty seats, spit-covered floors, and wild cursing and drinking disgusted genteel passengers, both black and white.

America had no legalized segregation yet. That would come after 1896, when "Jim Crow" laws were passed. But the Supreme Court of the United States had repealed the Civil Rights Act a year earlier. Now railroads throughout the South were trying "to draw the color line" by forcing African-Americans like Ida to ride in separate cars.

Legally, Ida was no longer a slave. Yet the savage acts that continued long after the Reconstruction years were another kind of enslavement. Lynchings spread like a disease in the 1880s and 1890s. Rates were especially high in rural areas where black people had recently settled. Whites convinced themselves that the newcomers were dangerous, and blacks were so few that they couldn't rely on one another for help. Evidence of the high rate of lynching in Ida's home state can be found in her diary: "13 colored men were shot down in cold blood yesterday in Miss.," she wrote in anguish. "O God when will these massacres cease."

Stories of brutality, then, were nothing new to Ida. The railroad's de facto segregation was just one more knot in a tangle of racial hatred, and she refused to be cowed. Like Rosa Parks, who would not give up her bus seat seven decades later in 1955, Ida would rather risk physical harm than submit to the indignity of discrimination.

The Chesapeake and Ohio Railroad had met its match. Ida knew she was a lady, and in the ladies' car she planned to stay! When the conductor grabbed her arm and pulled her out of the seat, she sank her teeth into the back of his hand. The poor fellow realized he couldn't handle her on his own, so he found two more men to haul her away.

Ida braced her feet against the seat in front and held on tight, but as white onlookers clapped their approval, she was dragged from the car. When the train stopped, she chose to leave rather than ride in the segregated smoker. The sleeves of her linen coat were torn out, and she later recalled that she "had been pretty roughly handled."

Ida was already bitter about her parents' deaths. She felt a "sense of injustice" over quitting school—fate had cheated her out of an education, and she sometimes "yearned with unutterable longing for the 'might have been.'" The orphaned young woman could not bring her parents back to life or reclaim her happy schoolgirl years. But she could harness her wrath to fight another kind of injustice. When she sued the railroad for forcing her to take unequal accommodations, the court awarded her five hundred dollars. Ida B. Wells was the first person since the repeal of the Civil Rights Act to sue in a state court for racial discrimination.

The railroad company appealed the decision the following year, and their lawyer offered her a series of bribes to "compromise" the case. Indignant, she refused but noted later that she would have been financially better off if she had accepted the money and agreed to give up the case.

Ida resented the lack of aid from the black community. "None of my people had ever seemed to feel that it was a race matter," she said in her autobiography, "and that they should help me with the fight." Even the traveling costs for the lawyer who represented her in the appeal came out of her own meager teaching salary.

If fellow blacks could not help Ida with money, they were still deeply interested in her court case. When the editor of the *Living Way,* a black Baptist newspaper in Memphis, asked her to write an article describing her experience, she was surprised. "I had no training," she recalled, "no literary gifts and graces." Yet this first article was so successful that the editor asked her to write more. Under the pen name "Iola" she contributed a series of weekly essays that she called "letters." Ida had never been afraid to speak her mind. Now she discovered that she had a writing voice, too.

Memphis, Tennessee
• December 1885–September 1887 •

While Ida waited for the appeal to creep through the court system, she found a teaching job in the city of Memphis. During this anxious waiting period, she comforted herself by keeping a diary. It seemed fitting to begin the diary on a visit to her old school in Holly Springs, Mississippi— "the land of my birth, the home of my nativity."

Going back to Holly Springs unlocked Ida's darkest memories. For seven years she had kept black thoughts tightly boxed inside her mind. Her grief over her parents' deaths was too sad to let out, her anger over her lost education too strong to control.

Now the diary let her release those feelings a little at a time. Ida wrote that she "visited the cemetery and found my father's and possibly my mother's grave and was present at a burying." She confined her sorrow to a few brief words— "came home very tired" and "the day has been a trying one to me"—but she had begun to face her past.

Ida also may have resurrected her greatest secret during her visit to the school. She glimpsed a man named "Prof. H." twice, and in the next paragraph she wrote of "old enemies" and "painful memories." The page that would explain these words is missing from Ida's dairy—taken, perhaps, by an older Ida or her grown daughter. After the missing page, the text resumes: ". . . and went to bid him goodbye. There was no reference to the past but he inquired solicitously concerning our welfare." Professor H. had been Ida's teacher. Was he one of her "enemies" or part of her "painful" past?

Six months later, Ida went back to Holly Springs to see friends graduate from the college. That night in her diary she recalled her broken dreams and admitted that Professor H. was the *real* reason she quit school. She wondered why he had "watched over and shielded" her friend, Annie, but had forsaken Ida years before. Then she compared herself with Annie, who had always been "obedient" and "easily controlled."

> Where I think of my tempestuous, rebellious, hard headed wilfullness, the trouble I gave, the disposition to question his authority—I remember that Mr. H. is but human and I no longer cherish feelings of resentment, nor blame him that my scholastic career was cut short; my own experience as a teacher enables me to see more clearly and I know that I was to blame.

Had she been rude to Professor H. when she was in school? Was she so rebellious that she had failed some of her courses? Despite the clues that Ida left in her diary, the answer may be gone forever, thrown away with the missing page.

Whatever the connection between Professor H. and quitting school, telling this crucial secret to the diary helped Ida understand her cantankerous self. Feeling angry was inevitable for the young woman who had lost so much when death took her parents. Getting mad, though, was not always the best route to getting what she wanted—as she had already learned, it could destroy the things she most desired.

After she confessed the secret about quitting school, she

began to counsel herself in the diary, praying "to better control my temper" and "to be more thoughtful and considerate in speech." For the rest of her life, Ida struggled to channel her anger in constructive ways. She often failed. But during the coming anti-lynching campaign, she managed to turn outrage into gritty determination. And it was Ida, not the obedient Annie, who fearlessly told the world about lynching.

Ida's small, four-inch-wide notebook reveals that the two diary-keeping years from 1885 to 1887 were a pivotal time in her life. Over two hundred pages of cramped script trace her growth from a grieving, vulnerable young woman to a professional journalist with a daring voice. The process was complicated, though. How could she reconcile everything she *had* to do with what she *wanted* to do?

Twenty-three-year-old Ida felt that she had to be a responsible mother and father to her own siblings. Although they didn't live with her, they considered her the head of the family and came to her for money and advice. She even thought of her "wild and reckless" brother, Jim, as her son. "I can get along well enough with other boys," she confessed to her diary, "but am too hasty & impatient with my own."

Motherhood (and sisterhood) were the domestic domain of a good woman. Sadly, Ida was trapped by its demands for self-sacrifice. She was expected to be a nurturing caregiver when, in some ways, she was still a needy child herself.

As many young women would, she savored the attention of a steady stream of men whom she said "idolized" her. Several wanted to marry her, but Ida was already burdened by parenthood and refused. Still, she enjoyed "an abundance of company" and played a courtship game as elaborate as a bustle on a dress. She gave her picture to suitors (similar to exchanging telephone numbers today), wrote flirty letters, pouted, promised affection, then withdrew it. Ida could be so coy that one young man said he felt that he was "in a tight jacket" in her presence.

And she made sure she looked fetching for male visitors. Ida adored pretty clothes. She could not resist spending fifteen dollars for a cloak or buying a new silk dress that cost too much. "My expenses are transcending my income," she once chided herself after a shopping spree. "I must stop. . . . It seems as if I should never be out of debt."

Despite her many admirers, she admitted she had trouble making real friends: "I have not kept the friends I have won but will try from this on," she promised her diary. Even friendships with other women seemed impossible. "Mrs. Rice . . . hopes in me to find a friend," Ida wrote early in her diary. "I wonder if her hopes will be blasted?"

There were other struggles as well. She longed to continue her studies, but did not know what books to read or "where to obtain the knowledge." And though teaching duties devoured most of her time, she blamed herself for "drifting along with no visible improvement."

As Ida wrestled with conflicting feelings of guilt and desire, kindness and contempt, doubt and determination, the diary became her referee. Sometimes she did not understand herself at all. "I don't know what's the matter with me," she wrote. "I feel so dissatisfied with my life, so isolated from all my kind. . . . My life seems awry, the machinery out of gear & I feel there is something wrong."

Some of Ida's difficulty came from nineteenth-century pressures to be a perfect woman. She wholeheartedly accepted the role, admiring a "truly noble-minded woman" in her diary. Part of this identity began at church, where restrictions on women's lives were reinforced from the pulpit. Once she received a "severe lecture" from older male members of her church for attending plays—loose behavior for a proper young lady. "I regretted it more than I can say," Ida confessed to her diary, "although I do not so keenly see the wrong."

And there was a racial ingredient, too. In December 1885, the same month she began her diary, she published an article called "Women's Mission." The essay preached that black women "have not awakened to a true sense of the responsibilities that devolve on them, of the influence they exert." Placing a heavy burden on herself and her sisters, Ida felt that the reputation of the race depended solely on the spotless behavior of black women. How else could they avoid sexual slurs like "wench" and "Jezebel"—labels freely used by the white men who had taken advantage of them during slavery?

Ida knew her reputation as a pure lady was her only currency. It was the one thing of value in a world that granted her no political power (she couldn't vote) and no economic power (she was paid less than either black or white men for her teaching job). A year into her diary, she published an essay telling women to "guard [their] virtue and good name" as "a miser hoards and guards his gold."

Quite naturally, then, Ida obeyed the rules of behavior that guaranteed purity: "Right here comes my temptation to flirt with him; to make him declare himself and forget all others," she told her diary of a suitor, "but I cannot—I will not consider it." To protect her "stainless" character, she kept an emotional distance from her many male friends.

And if she forgot to be strict with herself and the young men, her diary policed her behavior: "I blush to think I allowed him to caress me," she wrote. Two kisses "blistered" her lips and made her feel "humiliated" and "defrauded." Even when the "temptation of a lover" was "irresistible," Ida remained a good—and pure—young woman.

Memphis, Tennessee
· *"Brilliant Iola"* ·

During the two diary-keeping years, Ida's competence as a journalist emerged. Her personal writing helped her develop subject matter and a literary style for the public. The plain language of the novel *Ivanhoe* was charming, Ida told her diary. She also admired a sermon delivered in a "simple style." After considering these techniques, she decided to write her articles in a "helpful way" for former slaves who were just learning to read. She later said in her autobiography that she never "used a word of two syllables where one would serve the purpose."

As she entered the professional world of journalism, the diary also helped her leave the restrictive rules of domesticity behind. The ideal of the perfect woman began to crumble after the Civil War. War casualties had reduced the number of men available to fill jobs, while an increasingly industrialized economy had created new jobs. Woman's sphere expanded when middle-class women attended college or filled vacancies in factories, offices, and classrooms. As women became secretaries, librarians, or teachers, though, the jobs were "feminized," or reduced to lower status and lower pay.

Female abolitionists had learned the power of organized protest against slavery before the Civil War. Now they and their daughters were shocked to see all women, black and white, left out of the campaign for black male suffrage. "Do you believe the African race is composed entirely of males?" a women's rights advocate demanded to know. They continued their efforts to fight for the vote and to cure the enormous inequities caused by a changing economy, which put immense wealth in the hands of a few but left many others poor and illiterate.

By the 1880s, these activists were called "New Women." Typically they chose independence over marriage and worked for society as a whole instead of for a family. College-educated women like Jane Addams, Susan B. Anthony, and Frances Willard started settlement houses, campaigned for women's suffrage, and preached against alcohol abuse.

Dedicated women like Mary McLeod Bethune, Mary Church Terrell, and Anna J. Cooper became the New Women of the African-American community. To "uplift the race," they established black schools and performed community services through a growing network of black women's clubs. They too campaigned for temperance and women's right to vote, though they were often excluded from white women's organized protests.

With the help of her diary, Ida embraced the New Woman's role as reformer. She had a fearless ability to tell the truth, though she once wondered in her diary, "What is it that keeps urging me to write?" Her fame as a journalist spread throughout the black press, and soon she was known as the "Brilliant Iola."

Most of her early articles have disappeared. But titles mentioned in her diary—"Our Shame," "What Lack We Yet?" and "Our Young Men"—show that diary writing sharpened her editorial pen, turning private anxiety about being a woman and being black into public essays.

In September 1886, for instance, she read that a black woman in Tennessee had been blamed for a white woman's death. The woman was "taken from the county jail and stripped naked," Ida reported to her diary, "and hung up in the courthouse yard and her body riddled with bullets and left exposed to view."

The young correspondent responded to the hideous act with a violent editorial in a Tennessee newspaper, "almost advising murder!" It was typical of Ida to speak out first and worry later. "It may be unwise to express myself so strongly," she admitted to her diary after writing the editorial, "but I cannot help it."

Ida still fought to control her angry temperament, but that was difficult in these violent times for black Americans. Sometimes hot words of fury seemed to ignite the pages of her diary: "My blood was a'fire"—"I burned for revenge"— "my blood boils," she wrote. In another entry, she was "strongly tempted to say" that "killing was justifiable" if a woman's reputation was made the "jest & byword of the street."

As she struggled to cope with the almost unbearable tension of being African-American in a hostile South, she used her diary to form a philosophy of conflict. "God is over all & He will, so long as I am in the right, fight my battles, and give me what is my right," she decided. Ida's belief sustained her through the racial strife she faced in the coming years, though eventually she could only think of herself as always at war and "always in the right."

Memphis, Tennessee
• 1886–1892 •

During the 1886–1887 school year, Ida attended a wedding almost every month. She was the last single teacher left at her school and felt "singularly lonely & despondent." But she still resisted the idea of marriage. Like other professional New Women, she decided to put her energy into a blossoming career instead of a family.

She continued to teach, but considered it only one step above "menial" work. Journalism was her true love, and as teaching grew more boring, newspaper work became more exciting. She recalled in her autobiography that writing gave her a way "to express the real 'me.' "

The pending resolution of the railroad company's appeal also distracted her from thoughts of marriage. The case had been postponed for over a year. Now Ida nervously waited for April, when the state Supreme Court would decide if her victory would stand.

When the announcement finally came, Ida was so disappointed that a week passed before she could admit the painful news to her diary. Even then, it was difficult to face her feelings. She buried the information in an entry that began with, "Nothing of special interest to record from the past week," and ended with a reminder to buy stamps.

"The Supreme Court [of Tennessee] reversed the decision of the lower court in my behalf, last week," she wrote. A majority of judges had voted that the smoking car was equal to the ladies' car. The purpose of Ida's suit was "to harass," they said. She wrote in dismay, "I had hoped such great things from my suit for my people generally."

Ida rarely mentioned the rich oral black culture that surrounded her when she was growing up. Former slaves often rejected all reminders of their bondage, including the songs and stories of that era. But now she turned to the old tale about flying back to Africa to express her discouragement. "If it were possible," she wrote, "[I] would gather my race in my arms and fly far away with them."

Almost immediately after the decision, Ida used the diary to turn her helpless anger into resolve. "The Negro is beginning to think for himself," she declared the next day, "and consequently for him is to be found only unity." She was inspired by "the men of the race who do think." And soon Ida would join them, becoming one of those who "put their thought in action."

In July 1887, Ida celebrated her twenty-fifth birthday. The occasion made her feel old and wise: "Within the last ten [years] I have suffered more, learned more, lost more than I ever expect to, again." As she thought about the "Last Decade," she realized that she had "only begun to live—to know life as a whole with its joys and sorrows."

Looking back at her life helped Ida step forward into the world of journalism. In 1887 the editor of the Negro Press Association offered to pay her one dollar a week to write for the American Baptist Home Missionary Society. Shortly before her diary ended in September that year, she attended a convention of the Negro Press Association as their first woman representative.

The trip was a huge success. She delivered a paper, gave a speech, and met "many men of prominence." And when they elected her secretary, she felt that her fellow journalists had given her a "hearty welcome" to the field.

Ida had come a long way since the day she wrote in her diary that she was only a "defenseless girl." Though she still lost some battles with her anger, she was no longer just a furious young woman who blamed her troubles on "others who were brighter in color and withal prettier." Her writing, both private and public, had given her a way to channel her strong emotions toward a professional goal. It also gave her a satisfying new identity. Now she was called the "Princess of the Press."

"Since the appetite grows for what it feeds on," she later wrote, "the desire came to own a paper." By 1889, Ida owned one third of a black newspaper in Memphis, *Free Speech and Headlight*. Determined to "never tie" herself down to school-teaching, Ida decided to earn a living as a full-time writer in 1891. That summer she put on her traveling shoes and sold *Free Speech* subscriptions in little towns all over the Mississippi Valley.

Later Ida proudly remembered she had almost replaced her teaching salary within nine months. Once she collected so many silver dollars that she had to deposit them in a bank because the money bag was too heavy to carry. Concerned about her readers, she had the *Free Speech* printed on pink paper so a newly literate public could recognize the easy-to-read newspaper. In less than a year she increased circulation from fifteen hundred to four thousand subscribers. The "Princess of the Press" was ready for the grim crusade that lay ahead.

Memphis, New York, Chicago
· *1892–1931* ·

*I*da was visiting Natchez, Mississippi, when she heard the cruel news. Thomas Moss, a dear friend and father of her godchild, had been brutally lynched.

The incident began with a children's game of marbles in front of Thomas's grocery store. The game became a scuffle between black and white boys, and the scuffle turned into a fight. When adults joined in, violence flared.

That night white men broke into the back of Thomas's store. Armed black guards shot the intruders, and Thomas and his two partners were arrested along with over one hundred other black men. On Tuesday, March 8, 1892, a white mob kidnapped the three owners of the grocery store from the Memphis jail. They took Thomas and his co-workers "a mile north of the city limits" and shot them.

Ida recalled that Thomas Moss's death "changed the course" of her life. This was Memphis's first illegal execution since the Civil War, but lynching was common throughout the country, especially in the South.

Many people, including Ida's good friend Frederick Douglass, accepted the widespread myth that lynchings were the result of black men attacking white women. But Ida did not believe that "threadbare lie." Two months after Moss's lynching, she published an editorial in the *Free Speech*. She maintained that simple jealousy over black economic success fueled the brutal shootings and hangings of black people, and she used Thomas Moss's death as an example.

Ida left for New York City three days before the editorial appeared. The day after publication, a mob destroyed the newspaper office and left a note that threatened to hang her in front of the courthouse. When she heard the news, she didn't want to risk the lives of black men who would defend her if she went back to Memphis. Ida decided to stay in New York and lead her anti-lynching campaign from there.

Beginning in 1892, she published essays and pamphlets on lynching, including a one-hundred-page booklet that documented the history of lynching since the Emancipation Proclamation: *A Red Record: Tabulated Statistics and Alleged Causes of Lynchings in the United States*. The booklet was the result of months of research. Ida traveled to lynching sites, interviewed witnesses, and examined newspaper files for seven hundred and twenty-eight lynchings.

She concluded that only one third of the victims were accused of rape, and that few of those were guilty of the crime. Other flimsy reasons given for lynchings included prejudice, quarreling, and "making threats." Even women and children were lynched, Ida argued, disproving the fabrication about rape.

Determined to tell the world what she had discovered, she traveled thousands of miles and delivered hundreds of lectures to organize for passage of an anti-lynching law. Being around Ida during these years was like hearing someone yell

"Fire!" The shriek was alarming, but it forced people into action.

In 1895, Ida somehow found time in her exhausting schedule to marry Ferdinand Barnett, a journalist with a sense of humor that balanced her intensity. The only traditional thing about their marriage was Ida's white satin wedding dress trimmed with chiffon and orange blossoms. She hyphenated her name, returned to work on the Monday morning after the wedding, and turned all housekeeping duties over to her mother-in-law.

Ferdinand and Ida had four handsome children—two boys and two girls. Despite her misgivings about motherhood, she was surprised to find that she enjoyed her babies. When the National Association of Colored Women held their first historic meeting in 1896, Ida's six-month-old son came along. "I honestly believe that I am the only woman in the United States," she recalled in her autobiography, "who ever traveled throughout the country with a nursing baby to make political speeches."

As her children grew older, Ida tried to retire from public life four times. But she always found herself back at her writing desk or behind a podium. When she and Ferdinand moved to Chicago, they were the first to integrate their white neighborhood. She was furious when she saw that African-American migrants from the South were not allowed to stay at the YMCA or local hotels. Following the example of Jane Addams, who had founded Hull Settlement House for new immigrants, Ida established the Negro Fellowship League—a dormitory, reading room, and employment office for black newcomers to Chicago.

She also worked for equal rights for black soldiers during World War I and joined several marches in Washington for women's suffrage. Ida just could not pass up the chance to fight discrimination. Unfortunately, she did not know when to take the boxing gloves off.

When she began her campaign against lynching, she was a lone figure, the only one with enough courage to break the sexual taboo and talk about rape. As the civil rights movement grew larger, though, she found it impossible to compromise with other black leaders. Ida had always been rigid in her beliefs, but as she grew older, it became even more difficult to bend. She publicly disagreed with other African-Americans in the Equal Rights League, the National Association for the Advancement of Colored People, and the National Association of Colored Women. Eventually they ignored Ida and her abrasive opinions. Outrage had made her tough as a young woman, but in the end it paralyzed her as a leader.

When Ida B. Wells-Barnett died of uremic poisoning on March 21, 1931, she left a legacy of important "firsts." She was the first black woman journalist to tackle controversial issues inside the black community. She was also the first person to suggest that fear of black economic power was the real reason behind lynching. The first woman probation officer in Chicago, she founded that city's first black women's political club, the Alpha Suffrage Club.

In 1887, after the court had reversed Ida's victory over the railroad company, she had despaired in her diary, "O God is there no redress, no peace, no justice in this land for us?" Ida spent the rest of her life answering the question she asked in her diary. An anti-lynching bill never passed in Congress, but thanks to her efforts, public outcry greatly reduced the number of lynchings. In 1941 the city of Chicago changed the name of a housing project to the Ida B. Wells Homes. In a tribute to Ida's bold voice, her diary is buried in the cornerstone.

CHARLOTTE PERKINS GILMAN

· · · · ·

"The Princess Charlotte"

🌿

· *1860–1876* ·

Charlotte Perkins looked down from the top of the four-story staircase with a cherubic smile. There, on the ground floor far below, was a prime target—a bald spot on top of the landlady's head. Charlotte rolled a bit of spit around in her rosebud mouth, took aim, and—bull's-eye! The white glob landed smack in the middle of the woman's crown.

With a face like an angel, little Charlotte was used to being forgiven for her devilish pranks. But this time she must have let out a giggle, for a painful punishment followed her crime. "Hold out your hand!" her father commanded when he visited that night. Then Frederick Perkins beat her tiny palm twice with a small whip. Mary Perkins, her strict mother, had bought the whip for this exact purpose. If severe lectures could not cure her daughter of playing pranks, perhaps the sting of a lash would.

Charlotte's childhood mutiny was just one marker on the road to discovering her own voice. As she passed from girlhood through her twenties, she overcame the barriers of her mother's disapproval, a devastating mental illness, a broken marriage, and public censure. Finally, at the age of thirty, she found the life of independence that she desperately needed.

Born in 1860, Charlotte Perkins Gilman became a leading feminist and lecturer by the turn of the century. She developed pioneering theories on child care and was the author of a classic book on women and work. She also created a literary masterpiece, "The Yellow Wallpaper." Perhaps her greatest contribution was the idea that men and women share both feminine and masculine qualities. This was a radical thought in the era of the true woman—a rebellion against rigid definition of the sexes that was years ahead of its time.

Rebellion came easily to Charlotte as a child. Spitting on the landlady's head was her most daring act, she later remembered, but she and her brother, Thomas, also did "horrid things" to the woman's "red-eyed poodle, Pinky." She recalled standing on the sidewalk with Thomas, both of them squirting mouthfuls of water onto passersby, including the town mayor. Worst of all, they rolled giant hoops in mud, then splashed the brown stuff on passing ladies' wide skirts.

As Charlotte grew older, however, she learned to subdue her mischievous spirit and submit to the wishes of her cold mother. What else could she do? Frederick Perkins had abandoned his family when Charlotte was three years old, so she could not depend on him to soften her mother's demands. "My childhood had no father," Charlotte recalled later in her autobiography. She saw him so few times while growing up that she had exactly five memories of him—including the time he whipped her hand.

Nor could she turn to her father's relatives for comfort. Charlotte was proud that her father's old New England family was well educated, cultured, even famous (her great-aunt, Harriet Beecher Stowe, wrote the anti-slavery best-seller *Uncle Tom's Cabin*). But when Frederick left his wife and children, his relatives unfairly blamed Mary Perkins for *his* neglect. After she divorced him, they withdrew all financial support. Mary and her children moved nineteen times in eighteen years, always struggling for rent, clothing, and food.

Thomas was no help, either. He and Charlotte clung to each other for companionship and wicked fun during their unstable childhoods. He secretly feared, though, that his sister was smarter, and he tortured her with teasing. "Thomas was just unbearable today," Charlotte wrote in her diary at fifteen. "Sometimes I almost detest him." She also resented the privileges and freedom that her brother received simply because he was a male child. "Mother wouldn't let me go to Sunday School. Thomas invited out. *I wasn't!*" she jealously wrote.

Charlotte's one source of love, then, was her mother. Even that affection was doled out in stingy rations. Mary Perkins had "suffered so deeply" when her husband left that she could not spare any warmth for her daughter. She had married the wrong man, and she never forgave Charlotte for it. "I used to put away your little hand from my cheek when you were a nursing baby," she told her grown daughter years later. Hugs, kisses, compliments, even birthday celebrations were as rare as roast chicken in Charlotte Perkins's childhood.

The best way to avoid her mother's quick disapproval was to obey quietly. When Charlotte was thirteen, her mother insisted that she gave up her "chief happiness"—a rich fantasy life. Since the age of eight, she had created a make-believe world every night before going to sleep, and she hoarded these daydreams like fine chocolates.

Each evening as Charlotte lay in bed, she thought of "pleasant things." Once a week she allowed herself to imagine "lovelier, stranger things," and once a month she let herself create a "wonder." And one glorious time each year she indulged in a "fancy" about anything she wanted! She filled a notebook with some of these fairy-tale "fancies" and gave it a grand name:

Poetess
Literary and Artistic Vurks [Works]
of the Princess Charlotte

As Mary Perkins watched her daughter begin the journey to physical maturity, she might have feared that Charlotte's childhood fantasies would turn into the natural sexual feelings of a woman. So night after night, Charlotte followed her mother's wishes. She climbed into bed, "shut the door on happiness," and extinguished the one source of light in her dull, impoverished life. As Charlotte later remembered, "obedience was Right."

On the outside, Charlotte seemed to accept her mother's endless edicts. After turning fifteen, though, one incident revived the disobedience of her early childhood years. In October 1876, Mary Perkins wanted her daughter to apologize for something Charlotte swore she had not done. "You must do it," her mother commanded, "or you must leave me."

In a great spasm of rebellion, Charlotte spat out, "I am not going to do it. And I am not going to leave you." Afraid to take any further risk, she finished the angry statement in her head: "And what are you going to do about it?" Enraged by her loss of control over Charlotte, Mary struck her daughter.

The adult Charlotte later claimed, "I did not care in the least." If the blow did not physically hurt, it surely caused great emotional pain. The slap was a reminder that Mary Perkins dutifully fed, clothed, and taught her daughter as best she could—but she refused to provide the warm love that her child craved.

Charlotte remembered the confrontation as one of the "major events of a lifetime." She learned that no one could *make* her do anything she did not want to do. Charlotte said of the experience, "I was born." And standing up to her mother readied her for the next step toward an independent life: keeping a diary.

Providence, Rhode Island
· *1876* ·

*F*or Christmas 1875, Thomas presented fifteen-year-old Charlotte with an "Excelsior" diary, a record-keeping notebook that allowed eight lines per day. As usual, Thomas gave the diary to his sister as a competitive taunt rather than a fond gift: If Charlotte wrote something in her diary every day, Thomas would pay her one dollar at the end of the year.

Soon the diary became her secret escape route. When Mary Perkins left her daughter at home "to sew and set the table," Charlotte told the diary what *really* happened: "I *don't* sew but pop corn." When Thomas drove her crazy, she complained in secret: "T. needs squashing." When Mary moved her family two more times that year, the diary let Charlotte transport herself to a world of *her* choosing. Now she could break her mother's rule about daydreaming, and nobody but the diary would know.

Throughout 1876 Charlotte had delicious fantasies about Willie Dobol, an actor in a local theater. It was much more pleasant to moon over Willie in *As You Like It* than to think about "imbecilic" Thomas or the never-ending housework she had to do. "And *I'm going!!* Just think of it!" Charlotte gushed about her plans to see Willie in the play. "It's too lovely to happen! To sit and see him for a whole evening! I can't believe it possible!" She even found a dark blue handkerchief that belonged to the actor—"creased and soiled where *he* wore it!"

To please her mother, Charlotte had shut the door two years earlier on her "dear, bright, glittering dreams." Now the diary let them back in. Every time she wrote about "Sweet William," she broke her mother's rule about fantasy. And one night Charlotte indulged in the most forbidden act of all—lying in bed and thinking about Willie, she fantasized herself "into a state of beatitude before going to sleep."

There was one secret, though, that Charlotte could barely admit to herself or her diary—how much her father's rejection hurt. Frederick Perkins showed little love for his children. When Charlotte once pleaded with him to visit Thomas, who was seriously ill, he answered that he would come only "if necessary."

Frederick did love books and writing, however. So his daughter managed to pry attention from him with a literary shoehorn. She knew if she asked him for reading lists or advice on her education, he would respond. In February 1876 they met at the library in Providence, perhaps to discuss books. She had not seen him in years. "Saw father. Had a nice long talk," Charlotte reported to the diary. "Called me 'my child.' So nice."

This was all the young woman could bear to write. Years later she admitted that when she greeted her father with a kiss, he pushed her away and said she should not show affection in public. The adult Charlotte remembered she was treated like a "mere caller," and she vowed she would never kiss him again unless asked.

Still, a father is an important person in a girl's life, whether he is a good parent or bad, at home or away. Charlotte secretly pined for a loving father, even as he ignored her. The last entry for 1876 betrays her confused feelings about Frederick Perkins. "What a wasted year. But I don't know. Father has come home." Frederick did not live with his family, yet Charlotte thought of her home as his. In her mind, then, she was always watching at the window for her absent parent to return. And as children often do, she may have wrongly blamed herself when he did not appear.

Providence, Rhode Island
• *1877–1879* •

The diaries that Charlotte kept during her older teen years were a simmering soup of guilt, anger, resentment, and grief. Sometimes she let strong feelings bubble to the surface, though she usually hid them between the lines of the diary, not in the actual words. The family was pathetically dependent on Frederick Perkins for money, and Charlotte was crestfallen when he let them down, yet she kept her comments as brief as possible. "Letter from father. No spring clothes for us," she wrote. "Letter from father. Despondent." "Letter from father. He sends only thirty [dollars]."

Why did Charlotte avoid raging at her father's neglect in the diary? Perhaps she was following her mother's example. Apparently Mary Perkins seldom criticized the irresponsible Frederick. Despite the divorce, she loved him until the day she died. She was "as loyal as a spaniel to him," Charlotte said with contempt many years later. And if the abandoned mother accepted her lot, how could the abandoned daughter complain?

Eventually Charlotte *did* complain. Twenty years later she turned the trickle of terse sentences into a river of ideas on parenting, family organization, and child care. She wrote fifteen books and hundreds of magazine articles and delivered countless public lectures to protest a society that kept women at home, dependent on their husbands for money and imprisoned by household drudgery. This last was especially important.

Getting mad at her parents in the diary may have been taboo, but griping about housework was not. Charlotte's girlhood diaries witnessed the hidden tyranny of the "woman's sphere," and twenty years later she converted her frustrations into the theme of her book *Women and Economics:* Women who are dependent on their husbands, she wrote in 1898, could too easily be subordinated into household servants. And as Charlotte's diary revealed, so could daughters.

As overworked as Cinderella, the young woman sometimes did household tasks until her back ached, from "7 til
five." While Thomas Perkins went walking or fishing or to
school in Worcester, his sister stayed behind to clean silver,
make bread, scrub floors, iron, sweep, and sew. "Thomas
comes home at 7 A.M. Mother & I cook & labor," she wrote
at sixteen.

Even when Mary had one of her frequent ailments, Charlotte, not Thomas, picked up the load. "Mother has a bad
headache. I do all the work and iron," she fretted in her diary.
"Thomas goes out no one knows whither." Brought up to
believe in women's domestic destiny, Mary Perkins passed
"women's work" on to Charlotte as if it were a natural inheri-
tance, like her straight hair and brown eyes.

Even while Charlotte was a serving girl to the male member
of her household, she was as dependent as a pet on him. He
was a diversion from her dreary routine: *"Tommis is come!"*
she crowed when he came home from school in the spring of
1878, "Tommis is here!" When he returned in the fall, though,
he left Charlotte behind with two weeks of laundry as her only
entertainment. "All Thomas' horrible clothes to be washed &
boiled besides," she glumly noted in her diary.

Charlotte's girlhood diaries etched upon her memory a
skewed world where sons went away to school and daughters
stayed at home to do menial work. She never forgot the
injustices that she recorded in those pages. They laid the
foundation for her eventual argument that a husband and
wife should divide the work of the home equally for the good
of the whole family. "Whosoever, man or woman, lives always
in a small dark place," she later wrote, "will become inevita-
bly narrowed and weakened by it."

Before reaching this conclusion, however, she first had to free herself from her mother. That long process continued in her diary. One key event in the separation appears in her diary at the age of sixteen. The incident was so troubling that the writing was much messier and darker than usual—as if she were shoving the point of the pen into flesh instead of paper. She was so distraught that she even wrote the entry on the wrong day, then corrected it at the bottom of the page: "A Mistake. This is Wednesday."

What had so deeply disturbed Charlotte? "An invitation from Robert to a *college* concert & one from Edward to [Edwin] *Booth* in *Hamlet* & I couldn't accept either!" Charlotte wailed. "Mother didn't think twas best." Unable to release her iron control, Mary Perkins meant to keep her daughter at home under her "influence and management," if only to prove that she could. Charlotte's comment to her diary on the matter was short: "Oh dear! Oh dear!" but she later said that "something broke" inside her.

However, "oppression produces rebellion." Using the diary, young Charlotte found ways to defy her mother in secret. Fantasies about Willie gave way to an actual flirtation with her "homely" kissing cousin, Arthur. To protect her thoughts, she wrote her entries in shorthand so that no one could read about her shy, awkward relationship with him. (Years later she tried to read the shorthand entries, but she had forgotten the meaning of the outdated symbols.)

And her drawing ability gave her another way to resist her iron-willed "chère Mama." Mary Perkins usually scoffed at Charlotte's attempts to invent a new "coiffure." "Pull over my hair in search of a new style but mother doesn't like this," Charlotte wrote at seventeen. "Put up my hair in twist, comb, and two puffs. I think it's pretty. Mother don't," she sighed at eighteen.

Every time Charlotte created a hairdo, her mother disapproved. Each time Charlotte drew a profile of her head with a froth of curls gathered in some new style. The diary sketches let Charlotte confirm her own sense of style without having to say the words. And if she could not openly disagree with her mother, at least she could draw a scowling picture of her, complete with crocodile tears rolling down the page. Shorthand and secret drawings were not a full-scale revolt against Mary Perkins's control, but they kept Charlotte moving in that direction.

Providence, Rhode Island
• *1879–1881* •

*C*harlotte felt mixed up about boys and sex. The tall, scrawny young woman craved callers and valentines and wanted "a feller" of her own. Yet she thought that girls should be straightforward with boys, so her attempts at flirting fell flat. Then a Christmas visit in 1880 with cousins in Cambridge, Massachusetts, let her enjoy the "solid comfort" that had been missing in her life. "I never was so courted and entertained and amused & done for in all of my life," she exulted in the diary. One boy's attention left her nearly speechless: "The—the—why to think of its [*sic*] being *me!*"

Once she caught a boy's interest, though, she was terrified of it. When a distant cousin, Robert, attempted a "mild embrace," nineteen-year-old Charlotte rushed to tell her diary. "*First* time from *any* man!" she exclaimed. "Quench his

advances with much coolness." After an "uncuddled childhood," she was not used to physical contact—the mere
touch of the young man's arm made her "feel very dirty and
ashamed." In turn, boys were "afraid of her" and thought she
was "too smart."

Still, the many hours she spent with young men replaced
the male companionship that she missed from her father.
And the easy familiarity of skating, sleighing, and dancing
parties provided relief from the "toil and moil" of housework. Often "filled with friskiness" after a day with friends,
Charlotte entertained herself with droll comments in the
diary: "Almy and his twin brother play a [piano] duet with
their noses!" "Jim was about as sociable as a Greek frieze!"
Although Mary Perkins was jealous of her daughter's exuber-
ant spirits, Charlotte's widening circle of friends and fun led
her to write in 1881, "I am very happy today."

For women of Charlotte's age, socializing with the opposite sex was essential preparation for marriage. Nineteenth-
century girls worked hard at finding a husband, as if making
a marriage were making a career. But Charlotte wasn't sure
she wanted the job. A casualty of her parents' ruined relationship, she was uncertain about men and marriage. And
what about her growing "desire to help humanity"?

Marriage wasn't her only choice, especially as more educa-
tional and job opportunities for women became available
during the 1880s, but it was the most respectable. Charlotte
had seen that a woman's commitment to a man meant full-
time service to him, his children, and his home. "Every man,"
she wrote years later, "requires one whole woman to minister
to him! There must be nothing left of her."

Charlotte saw herself as having "two opposing natures."

No wilting wisteria blossom, she was physically strong, tall, and smart—everything a man was supposed to be. All her life she had seen "womanly" and "manly" defined through advertising, newspaper articles, and women's magazines. With these images in her head, it never occurred to her that a "strong-minded" woman like herself could function as an intelligent being within marriage.

During the summer of 1881, she shared her confusion over marriage with her dear friend, Martha. In fact, Charlotte unconsciously made Martha into a substitute spouse. They had been friends for three years, and she saw her "little chick" almost every day. She wrote in her diary, "I love her," explaining years later that "this was love but not sex." With her friend, she knew "peace of mind, understanding, comfort, deep affection." In other words, every warm feeling that she missed in her mother and needed in a man.

Then Martha became engaged. "She hath a ring, I have a pain," Charlotte wept to her diary in November 1881. Abandoned yet again, she felt that she "had no one else." When 1881 ended, Charlotte reflected upon it as the year when she had lost a "perfect friendship."

Another event in 1881 was almost as important as losing Martha. With huge relief, Charlotte waved a flag of liberation in her diary: "This Year I attained my majority—may I never loose [lose] it!" Anticipating her July birthday, Charlotte began to celebrate in June. To the "chilly horror" of her mother, she wore a pink muslin dress when she felt like it, made a brown velvet hat she had wanted since she was fifteen, and even slipped a cameo ring on her engagement finger to "mystify all." The declarations of independence were tiny but triumphant.

And after turning twenty-one, she was legally free. Charlotte would no longer have to let Mother read her letters. No more would she dutifully report the who, what, and where of every event in her "handled" life.

In January 1882, two months after Martha's engagement, Charlotte met an artist named Charles Walter Stetson. After only six meetings in three weeks, he proposed, but she refused—she still had doubts about matrimony and a deep conviction that she should work for the "improvement of the human race." Yet his offer must have tempted her. After all, marriage would be a permanent escape from Mother.

Providence, Rhode Island
· *1882–1887* ·

The joy seemed to go out of Charlotte's diaries after Martha married. Compared with earlier years, only a few slubs of emotion surface in the endless details of her entries. Oddly, Charlotte was becoming more like her mother. Proud of her composure, she had tried since the age of fifteen to make herself numb. That way, she figured, she wouldn't feel the tug when Mother twisted the strings of her life.

What was *really* going on underneath the meals, chores, letters, and callers that made the fabric of her day? Now that she was legally free to come and go as she pleased, she realized she was still caught in an economic cage. Earning her own money had always been a thrill—"I'm a woman o'business!" she had squealed at fifteen after earning four dollars as a cashier.

Yet the income she made from giving art lessons and

selling hand-painted greeting cards would never be enough to let her move out on her own. She must have felt quite trapped. With no college degree or professional training, there was only one way to leave her mother's house: marriage.

Finally, Charlotte reluctantly agreed to wed Walter Stetson in May 1884. They loved each other, but uncertainty tormented her. "I anticipate a future of failing and suffering," she keened in her diary. "Children sickly and unhappy. Husband miserable because of my distress; and I ———!"

She busied herself with preparations for their wedding and new house. But even as she bought a ring, pillows, and slop jars, common sense told her this union would be a disaster. However, her mother had never taught her to believe in herself, so Charlotte could not trust her own thoughts now.

Mary Perkins was as bloodless as ever on the big day. "His parents kind and affectionate," Charlotte told her diary, "but mother declines to kiss me and merely says 'goodbye.' " It was a desolate send-off for the years ahead.

"I'm not domestic," Charlotte once told her friend Martha, "and I don't want to be." Even so, she sailed into an uneasy sea of domesticity when she married Walter Stetson. She was proud of her "delectable" dinners and "excellent breakfasts" but wearied of the "dishes, dishes, dishes!" It seemed perfectly logical to ask Walter to pay her for getting him "a nice little dinner." But the suggestion insulted him, and she felt guilty for asking. Nor did he like Charlotte's obvious enjoyment of sex. "I must keep more to myself," she rebuked herself in the diary, "and be asked." Instead of faulting society for making unreasonable rules for women, Charlotte blamed herself when she broke them.

They had been married less than a month when she began to feel "numb" and "helpless"—signs of her coming depression. After becoming pregnant, she felt even more hopeless and fatigued. "A sort of gray fog drifted across my mind," she later remembered, "a cloud that grew and darkened." Walter took over many of the household duties. But true to form, Mary Perkins left her daughter in the middle of a difficult pregnancy to visit Thomas in Utah. She was not present for baby Katherine's birth in March 1885.

Mary did return in time to make Charlotte feel utterly inadequate as a mother. Charlotte felt too sad to look after her infant daughter, so she was grateful when her mother could bathe and dress Katherine during the day. She secretly worried in her diary, though, that she "would forget how to take care" of her own child. Unable to please as a daughter, now Charlotte felt guilty because she thought she was a failure as a mother. "Every morning the same hopeless waking," she wrote a few months after Katherine was born, "Retreat impossible, escape impossible."

Like a storm waiting for the right winds to give it force, Charlotte's breakdown may have been inevitable. There was a history of manic-depressive illness in her mother's family, so a chemical imbalance may have caused her emotional difficulties. Changing hormone levels during pregnancy could also have induced her depression. Physical fatigue caused by a malfunctioning thyroid gland might have sapped her mental strength as well—she recorded in her diary that she took thyroid medication.

Most of all, though, her depressed state was due to loss of creativity. Charlotte wanted to be engaged with life, to be a "world helper," especially for women's rights. Sadly, neither she nor Walter could envision a married life where, like a man, she could mix marriage with parenting and a career.

For the next two years her symptoms disappeared when she traveled, when she exercised at the local gymnasium, while she was reading, or when she wrote for a woman's suffrage column in the Providence newspaper. But even with Walter's help, she felt "brainless" when faced with domestic duties that must have reminded her of her bleak childhood.

By the spring of 1887, Charlotte experienced frenzied bouts of hysteria. Fearful that she had "some brain disease," she traveled to see Doctor S. Weir Mitchell in Philadelphia, a physician noted for his "Rest Cure." She left her "old friend" the diary behind but wrote one last entry that brought her just to the edge of revolt.

As with her mother, guilt paralyzed Charlotte. She was unable to express anger aloud to Walter, yet she could speak to him sternly in the diary. "Learn to doubt your judgement," she warned him, "before it seeks to mould another life as it has mine." In a tone as cold as her mother's voice, she silently condemned her husband for failing to do what she should have done herself: listen to her doubts about marriage.

"I asked you a few days before our marriage if you would take the responsibility entirely on yourself," she reminded him in the diary. "You said yes. Bear it then."

Walter did not deserve all of Charlotte's unspoken anger. He too was a victim of rigid nineteenth-century traditions. Before they married, she had asked him if he would mind if she supported herself. Men were expected to provide for their families, and Walter thought the world would judge him inadequate if his wife earned her own money. Yes, he *would* mind, he told his bride-to-be. Now, though, Charlotte's illness made him feel that he had become a "mere instrument of money getting."

During their courtship, he had rejoiced in his diary that "she is willing to do anything, go anywhere, so long as I am with her." But after her breakdown, the chains of female/male roles bruised them both. Now Walter thought she was too "clinging" and "dependent." To be a good woman, Charlotte had obeyed too well her mother's and her husband's commands. The resulting illness was only a cruel exaggeration of what they insisted she become: silent, submissive, ashamed.

Philadelphia, Providence, Pasadena
· *1887–1889* ·

*T*wenty-six-year-old Charlotte hoped that her month-long stay at Dr. Mitchell's Philadelphia sanitorium would cure her depression, but his "Rest Cure" was a calamity. Rest was its main component, and she later remembered that she was kept in bed for a month, "fed, bathed, rubbed." Not allowed to sit up, sew, write, or read, she could only brush her teeth.

The treatment itself was "agreeable," she later said. Distance from her family, a major source of guilt, would have made her feel better for a time. And perhaps the three to four pints of milk that Mitchell prescribed for thin patients gave her strength—diary entries show that she had trouble maintaining a healthy weight.

But Mitchell believed that many depressed women were "malingerers" looking only for "sympathy" and "petty power." His final aim was to make sure a woman could go back to the domestic life, happy to continue her daily round of chores and child care. Like a prisoner relieved to be in a regular cell after solitary confinement, a woman would find housework attractive compared with the "bitter medicine" of the rest cure.

Mitchell sent Charlotte back to Providence with the command to "Live as domestic a life as possible. Have but two hours' intellectual life a day. And never touch pen, brush or pencil as long as you live." The very things that she needed— a chance to be creative and a sense of purpose beyond her home—were forbidden.

This sentence of execution almost drove Charlotte mad within a month. She "blankly" sat shaking her head back and forth, crawling into closets and under beds. Mindlessly she swatted a "rag baby" that hung from a doorknob—anything to ease the "nightmare gloom" of her mental anguish.

To save her sanity, Charlotte and Walter agreed to separate, then to divorce. Taking Katherine with her, she left Providence and moved to Pasadena, California, to be near her close friend Grace. "It was not a choice," she later said, "between going and staying, but between going sane and staying insane." In the "beauty" and "nerve-rest" of the California weather, Charlotte began to recover.

For the next three years, she was too weak to keep a diary. But when her separation became final in January 1890, Charlotte celebrated the beginning of her "first year of freedom" by buying a tiny notebook. The "scrappy little two by four diary" would make few demands on the diarist—just what she needed to prepare for her greatest act of emancipation: writing "The Yellow Wallpaper."

With every passing month of 1890, Charlotte used writing to move closer to her true self. Calmly, her own voice—not that of Mary Perkins, Walter Stetson, or Weir Mitchell—floated up from a quiet pool deep within. She recorded the process in the diary: By March she was sending plays, articles, and poetry to editors. In May she gloried in the "Great Success" of her first public lecture. September found her writing almost every day, and at the end of the year she realized that her "whole literary reputation had begun." This was "work, the normal life of every human being," she rejoiced. "Work, which is joy and growth and service, without which one is a pauper and a parasite."

Midway through the year, she untied the last bonds of restraint. She wrote a terrifying story for Dr. Mitchell, hoping it would "save people from being driven crazy." Based on her own brush with lunacy, "The Yellow Wallpaper" traces the road to madness. Like Charlotte, the depressed character of the story has a husband, a baby, and a doctor named Mitchell. He has prescribed a "rest cure" for her on an isolated country estate. As Charlotte described the hallucinations of a woman trapped inside a hideous, stinking wallpaper, she transformed her own tremors of insanity into unforgettable literature.

Eerily, the voice of the narrator echoes the weary voice in teenage Charlotte's diary. "Why I had nearly forgotten you my beloved diary & Fourth of July too," Charlotte wrote the day after her seventeenth birthday, "I celebrate by washing dishes and ironing." "Well, the Fourth of July is over!"

sighed the woman in the "Yellow Wallpaper"; "The people are all gone and I am tired out."

Charlotte sent the story as a message to Dr. Mitchell but never got a reply. A national magazine published it a year later, and then it was included in a collection of short fiction. After fifteen years of hidden rebellion in her diaries, at last Charlotte could openly condemn a society that kept women confined to a domestic life without choice.

Most important, "The Yellow Wallpaper" enabled her to release her anger toward the figures who had forced society's will upon her: her mother, husband, and doctor. Through fiction, she could safely descend into dark memory, confront her ordeal, and come out again to the light, to herself.

Oakland, California, and New York City
• 1891–1935 •

Although Charlotte said her illness left her mind "like a piece of boiled spinach," she became an amazingly productive writer after "The Yellow Wallpaper." Between 1898 and 1935, she wrote five major books on human rights issues, including child care and housework. Between 1909 and 1916 she produced her own magazine, *The Forerunner,* writing every word of every issue.

This new Charlotte was as disobedient as the old one had been compliant. Still uncomfortable with men, still straining to sort out her sexual feelings after the divorce, she may have had a love affair with a woman named Adele. "My last love," thirty-three-year-old Charlotte wrote in her diary when this relationship ended, "proves even as the others."

After Charlotte moved to Oakland, California, Mary Perkins learned that she had cancer and joined her daughter. So as Charlotte struggled to remain mentally well, she also nursed her dying mother. Unable to support Katherine and Mary with the few dollars earned from speaking and writing, she sent her nine-year-old daughter to live with Walter. Her former husband had moved to California too, and in a soap-opera turn of events married Charlotte's friend Grace. The arrangement suited everyone: the nurturing Grace was happy to raise Charlotte's child as her own, Walter was reunited with his daughter, and Katherine could live with both a mother and a father.

But the choice was so painful that thirty years later, Charlotte wept when she wrote about it in her autobiography. Still, she thought she was doing the best thing for her daughter. They remained in touch through letters and frequent visits until Katherine rejoined her mother at age sixteen. By now, though, Charlotte was a well-known figure, and her private life was open to criticism. Newspapers had already made a sensation out of her divorce. In 1892 an article in the *Boston Globe* described Charlotte as a "too practical wife" who had "ideas of her own." Now she again scandalized a public who expected a mother to raise her own child.

In 1900 Charlotte caused another stir when she remarried at the age of forty. Not only was Houghton Gilman seven years younger, he was her first cousin. Their family disapproved, but Charlotte happily disobeyed their wishes and moved to New York to be with him. She loved "Ho" too deeply to listen to any voice except her own.

He gave her the love and trust she had been seeking all her life, remaining a steadfast anchor throughout her writing and lecturing career. They shared a satisfying thirty-four-year marriage until his death in 1934. After a three-year battle with breast cancer, Charlotte chose to end her life on August 17, 1935.

Charlotte's exploration of the differences and likenesses between women and men was revolutionary for her time. From personal experience, she knew that a healthy society allowed women and men to develop *all* of their potential. Except for childbearing, men and women are much more alike than different, she said. Theorists are still trying to decide how much the sexes differ and why. As they struggle for answers, they have Charlotte's words to guide them: "The most important fact about the sexes, men and women," she wrote, "is the common humanity we share, not the differences that distinguish us."

Accounts and Memoranda

❧

*N*ineteenth-century diarists used the last page of their journals as a ledger or to contemplate the closing year. A final tally can be made for the diarists in *Keeping Secrets*, too. If you turn back to the table of contents, you will see a descriptive quotation next to every diarist's name. These labels are also repeated above the text in each chapter. They were given to the writers during their lifetimes. Together, they define the nineteenth-century female image. Words like "lady," "genteel," and "princess" show what family, ministers, friends, and the press saw when they looked at the seven women.

The excerpt printed next to each diarist's photograph shows how she viewed herself. Somewhere at the crossroad between others' expectations and her own honest reflection, each woman formed a new identity. Most became writers, and their literature, like a double mirror, reflects a hidden person first seen in the pages of a diary.

Perhaps none of the women could explain how a diary helped them become writers. For them and for young people who keep diaries now, the alchemy of discovering a secret self is wonderful but mysterious. What matters is the spell cast after a girl picks up a pen—when she decides, like

Charlotte Forten, that the "passing events" of her life "naturally possess great interest." Then she begins to make an image of her own. She can understand who she has been, search for the person she might become, and as one diarist wrote in 1917, finally "meet Me face to face."

Notes

❧

Dear Diary

Page 4: Often the writers openly revealed secrets in their diaries ("All this I tell *you,* Dear A., as a great secret"). But sometimes they hid secrets on purpose ("I feel MISERABLY both in mind and body and DARE NOT say another word to thee, my journal") or by accident. When I sensed secrets buried beneath the surface of the text, I investigated other sources for clues to what the diarist was hiding and why. The diaries of Kate Chopin, Alice Dunbar-Nelson, and Ida B. Wells were especially indirect. Speculations about their secrets—Kate's affair, Alice's unhappy first marriage, why Ida dropped out of school—are based on evidence in other diary entries, biographies, autobiographical writings, or their own published works.

Page 6: More information about the household division of labor can be found in *More Work for Mother,* Cowan, 26–31 and 63–68.

Page 7: To read further about the development of private and public spheres in the Victorian era, see *Born for Liberty,* Evans, Chapter 4.

Page 7: A history of the influential *Godey's Ladies Book* is in Chapter 5 of *Women and the American Experience,* Woloch. Such magazines had a huge readership and a strong influence on middle-class American society. The stories and articles reinforced the idea that as men went out into the world to compete and make money, women stayed at home to fulfill their domestic duty as the perfect wife, mother, daughter, or sister.

Page 7: "Working like nature" is from a poem by William Wordsworth requoted in *Dimity Convictions,* Welter, 29.

Pages 7–8: More painful details about corsets, bustles, petticoats, and high heels are in "Health in Body and Mind," *The Light of the Home,* Green.

Page 8: The rise of women's high schools and colleges is discussed in *Women and the American Experience,* Woloch, 276–83.

Louisa May Alcott

Page 11: All quotations from Bronson Alcott's diaries are from *The Journals of Bronson Alcott,* Shepard.

Page 12: By one estimate, *Little Women* sold over five million copies around the world by 1950. *Louisa May Alcott and "Little Women,"* Delamar, 162.

Page 13: For a discussion of Louisa as the "dutiful daughter," see "*Little Women:* The American Female Myth" in *Sister's Choice,* Showalter.

Page 15: Use of the royal "we" originated with "the divine right of kings," a doctrine defended by rulers who claimed their authority was transmitted directly through God.

Page 15: Unless otherwise noted, all quotations from Louisa May Alcott's diaries are from *The Journals of Louisa May Alcott,* Stern.

Pages 15–16: Quotations from Abba Alcott's diaries and letters are taken from *Louisa May,* Saxton, 32, 39.

Pages 16–17: More anecdotes about Louisa May Alcott's childhood can be found in *Louisa May Alcott,* Cheney.

Page 18: Bronson's impractical piety exasperated even his closest friends. Transcendentalist Margaret Fuller called him a man with one idea. After Emerson visited Fruitlands, he wrote in his diary, "Alcott and Lane [a British Transcendentalist] are always feeling of their shoulders to find if their wings are sprouting."

Page 18: Bronson's note to his daughter is quoted in *Louisa May,* Saxton, 137.

Page 21: Apparently Bronson Alcott's lectures were much more riveting than his writings. For a fictionalized description of his speaking style, see "Appendix B: Early Sketches by the Alcott Sisters" in *The Journals,* Stern, p. 339.

Page 22: A version of "The Masked Marriage" appears in the chapter of *Little Women* called "The P.C. and P.O."

Page 27: For more description of Louisa's two-week visit with Ladislas Wisniewski in Paris see *Louisa May,* Saxton, 289.

Pages 27–28: Louisa described the genesis of the character of Laurie in a letter quoted in *The Journals,* Stern, 148, n40.

Pages 28–29: For a detailed account of the discovery of the true identity of "A. M. Barnard," see the introductions by Stern to *Behind a Mask, From Jo March's Attic,* and *Plots and Counterplots.*

Page 33: For more discussion of nineteenth-century women writers' reluctance to live on their own, see *Private Woman, Public Stage,* Kelley, 179.

Charlotte Forten

Page 35: All quotations from the diaries of Charlotte Forten are from *The Journals of Charlotte Forten Grimké,* Stevenson.

Page 38: Louisa May Alcott mentions the "Burns mob" at the end of her 1854 diary. See *The Journals of Louisa May Alcott,* Stern, 72 and 72n.

Pages 39–40: An excerpt from Charlotte Forten's diary and some of her published poetry is in *Afro-American Women Writers,* Shockley, 75–83.

Page 41: When St. Helena was seized in 1862, former slaves were considered contraband, or illegal property, of the Confederates. Still not officially free, they were employed by the United States Army until the Emancipation Proclamation of January 1, 1863.

Page 43: For more information on Northern teachers who taught the freed people, see *Soldiers of Light and Love: Northern Teachers and Georgia Blacks,* Jones.

Pages 43–44: Charlotte's surroundings were not luxurious. The wide steps and broad front porch of Oaklands were imposing from the outside. But according to her diary, the inside was "rather desolate" and furnished with only "two bureaus, three small pine tables and two chairs, one of which has a broken back."

Page 44: Laura Towne's diary is quoted in *Rehearsal for Reconstruction,* Rose, 161.

Page 44: The letter to Garrison is quoted in *We Are Your Sisters,* Sterling, 280–81.

Page 44: Charlotte's comments sound condescending now, but she was four generations removed from her African heritage. Another seventy years would pass before linguists and anthropologists would recognize the African culture that had survived on the Sea Islands. Then, with the help of documents like Charlotte's diary, they proved that the Sea Islands were a rich pocket of language, music, art, and religion with an African flavor.

Page 44: For many years, scholars incorrectly considered the Gullah language spoken on the Sea Islands to be a corruption of lower-class white dialect. For a history of the Gullah language, see *Africanisms in the Gullah Dialect,* Turner.

Page 46: Colonel Robert Shaw and most of the 54th Regiment were killed when they tried to capture Fort Wagner, South Carolina.

Sarah Jane Foster

Page 53: Quotation is from "My Disappointment." For Sarah's other published poetry and stories, see *Sarah Jane Foster: Teacher of the Freedmen,* Reilly, Appendix.

Page 53: All quotations from Sarah's diaries and letters are from *Sarah Jane Foster,* Reilly.

Page 60: Historians are divided on whether the Northern teachers were meddling busybodies or helpful to the freed people. For a summary of the issue, read the introduction to *Sarah Jane Foster,* Reilly.

Page 60: Sarah's role as a "good" teacher and "dutiful daughter" is discussed in the Jacqueline Jones's foreword to *Sarah Jane Foster,* Reilly, vi.

Kate Chopin

Page 69: Kate wrote about climbing cherry trees with Kitty in a reminiscence reprinted in *A Kate Chopin Miscellany,* Seyersted, 104.

Page 70: Other anecdotes about Kate's girlhood are from Kitty Garesché's reminiscence in *Kate Chopin and Her Creole Stories,* Rankin, 36–37.

Page 71: Except for the New Orleans diary, all quotations from Kate Chopin's diaries are taken from *A Kate Chopin Miscellany,* Seyersted.

Page 75: When Kate wrote *The Awakening,* she used the word "alone" two dozen times according to Margo Culley, quoted in *Women on the Color Line,* Elfenbein, 143.

Page 76: The whereabouts of Kate's New Orleans diary is now unknown, although it was seen and summarized by Kate's first biographer in *Kate Chopin and her Creole Stories,* Rankin, 92.

Pages 77–78: Details about Kate's reception in Cloutierville are from an interview by the author with Amanda Chenault, a descendant of Kate's neighbor, Bayou Folk Museum, Cloutierville, Louisiana, June 30, 1933.

Page 78: Though the walls of the house were eighteen inches thick, the tropical summer heat was fierce. A *branlé* hung from the ceiling in the four main rooms of the Chopin home.

Page 79: Quotations are from interviews with descendants of Cloutierville residents in *Kate Chopin,* Toth, 460n.

Page 83: Details on African-Americans who lived in Kate's household when she was growing up can be found in *Kate Chopin,* Toth, 30.

Page 85: When Edna's husband confides in his doctor about her rebellious behavior, the doctor takes a typical nineteenth-century view: "Woman, my dear friend, is a very peculiar and delicate organism. . . . Most women are moody and whimsical." See *The Awakening,* Chopin, 71.

Page 87: Kate's use of the "Jezebel" stereotype of black women in "The Storm" is discussed in *Women on the Color Line,* Elfenbein, 121, 126, 141.

Page 87: According to Kate's son, Felix Chopin, the St. Louis public library banned *The Awakening* and removed it from the library shelves. This widely accepted story is refuted in *Kate Chopin,* Toth, Chapter 22.

Alice Dunbar-Nelson

Page 91: Alice's distinction as the first African-American woman to publish a book of short fiction is noted in *Afro-American Women Writers,* Shockley, 263.

Page 92: Alice discussed the definition of Creole in a 1916 article: A white man born in Louisiana would say that a Creole is white with French or Spanish ancestors. A person of color born in Louisiana would say that a Creole has "mixed strains of everything un-American, with the African strain slightly apparent." Quoted in "Race and Gender in the Early Works of Alice Dunbar-Nelson" by Bryan, *Louisiana Women Writers,* Brown and Ewell, 121.

Page 92: The color-caste system in New Orleans is further described in *Color, Sex & Poetry,* Hull, 35.

Page 93: The letter in which Alice tells the story of her mother's enslavement is reprinted in *Color, Sex & Poetry,* Hull, 33.

Page 93: The information on Alice's public school experience is from her essay "Brass Ankles Speaks," published for the first time in *The Collected Works of Alice Dunbar-Nelson,* Vol. 2, Hull, 317.

Page 94: The references to a diary are from *The Confessions of a Lazy Woman,* a manuscript in the special collection of the University of Delaware Library.

Page 94: Portions of four diaries by African-American women, including Ida B. Wells, were published for the first time in *We Are Your Sisters,* Sterling, Part VI.

Page 95: Further analysis of black women's diaries can be found in the introduction to *Give Us This Day: The Diaries of Alice Dunbar-Nelson,* Hull, 13–14.

Page 95: For more information on Alice and Paul's courtship through letters, see "The Dunbar Letters," Alexander, 24, and *Afro-American Women Writers,* Shockley, 264.

Page 97: Alice's criticisms of her manuscript are from *Color, Sex & Poetry,* Hull, 58. Alice's comments make it clear that she never regarded *Confessions of a Lazy Woman* as a real diary. The many parallels between the narrator's life and the author's life, though, support reading the novel as if it were a diary.

Pages 100–101: For more information on the breakup of the marriage, see *Color, Sex & Poetry,* Hull, 45.

Page 104: An analysis of Alice's literature in the context of the Harlem Renaissance can be found in the introduction to *Color, Sex & Poetry,* Hull.

Page 104: "Stones of the Village" was published for the first time in *The Collected Works of Alice Dunbar-Nelson,* Vol. 3, Hull, 3.

Page 105: Frances E. W. Harper hinted at the issue of "passing" but did not directly address it in her 1892 novel, *Iola Leroy.* The first published fiction by an African-American concerning the color line was the title story in *The Wife of His Youth and Other Stories,* by Charles Chestnutt, published in 1899.

Page 111: A full description of Alice's diaries is in *Give Us This Day,* Hull, 33.

Ida B. Wells

Page 113: All diary quotations are from Ida B. Wells's manuscript diary, Special Collections, Joseph Regenstein Library, University of Chicago.

Page 114: Slave marriages were not considered legally binding, so many African-American couples remarried after Emancipation.

Pages 114–116: The account of the death of Ida's parents, how she became head of the family, and the ensuing scandal is taken from *Crusade for Justice,* Duster, 10–17.

Page 115: Statistics about the yellow fever are from "Yellow Fever: Scourge of the South" in *Disease and Distinctiveness,* Carrigan, 66.

Pages 118–19: More details about the railroad's response to the repeal of the Civil Rights Act and background on lynching can be found in *The Promise of the New South,* Ayers, 156.

Page 120: The Civil Rights Act of 1875 had guaranteed equal rights to all African-Americans at the national level. Repeal of the act forced black people to take individual cases of discrimination to the state courts. Since Ida was the first to do so, Southern states worried that her victory would set a precedent for the outcome of later lawsuits.

Page 121: Anxious to hide secrets unbecoming to a good woman, nineteenth-century women often censored or destroyed their diaries. Louisa May Alcott's mother, Abba, used scissors to cut out all references to herself in her husband's diary. After Abba died, Louisa read and destroyed her mother's diaries and many of her own.

Page 122: Since we do not know how the missing diary page disappeared, we can only speculate that it contained the whole story about Professor H. Still; we can be sure that Ida was keeping a secret, since her heartfelt admission that she was "to blame" for quitting school is a clear contradiction to her autobiography. (The autobiography was edited by Ida's oldest daughter.)

Page 127: Ida was friends with several white women in the reform movement, especially Susan B. Anthony and Jane Addams. But she clashed with Frances Willard, head of the National Women's Temperance Union. Willard opposed giving the vote to "a plantation Negro who can neither read nor write, whose ideas are bounded by the fence of his own field and the price of his own mule."

Page 127: When the General Federation of Women's Clubs met in 1900, they denied a seat to Mary Church Terrell, who represented the National Federation of Colored Women.

Page 131: According to her autobiography, Ida received support and encouragement from black male journalists when she first entered the field. Later they often commented on her physical appearance and treated her as a peculiar exception rather than a colleague.

Page 134: The National American Woman Suffrage Association asked Ida not to march because she might offend Southern white women. She marched anyway.

Charlotte Perkins Gilman

Page 137: Charlotte recalled childhood pranks and conflicts with her mother in her autobiography, *The Living of Charlotte Perkins Gilman,* Gilman, Chapters 1–3.

Page 139: Quotations from Charlotte's 1876 diary are from *The Diaries of Charlotte Perkins Gilman,* Knight. All other diary quotations are from microfiche of Charlotte's diaries, Schlesinger Library, Radcliffe College.

Page 145: Charlotte addressed issues of men and women sharing housework in *The Home: Its Work and Influence,* Gilman (New York: Source Book Press, 1970).

Page 152: Charlotte's most recent biographer relates the family's history of manic-depression in *To Herland and Beyond: The Life and Work of Charlotte Perkins Gilman,* Lane, 110–12.

Page 152: Charlotte recorded in her diary that she took thyroid medication, indicating an over- or underactive thyroid gland. Too much or too little thyroxin, the hormone produced by the thyroid, can cause debilitating fatigue.

Page 157: The idea that "The Yellow Wallpaper" was a release of pent-up anger against Mary Perkins, Walter Stetson, and S. Weir Mitchell is from *To Herland and Beyond,* Lane, 128.

Memoranda

Page 161: "I meet Me face to face" is from a diary written for publication by Mary Maclane of Butte, Montana. Quoted in " 'I Look at Me': Self as Subject in the Diaries of American Women," *Women's Studies Quarterly,* 1989, 3 & 4, 15–23.

Bibliography

Books Cited in Text

Alcott, Bronson. *The Journals of Bronson Alcott.* Edited by Odell Shepard. Boston: Little, Brown, 1938.

Alcott, Louisa May. *The Journals of Louisa May Alcott.* Edited by Madeleine Stern. Boston: Little, Brown, 1989.

——. *Louisa May Alcott: Her Life, Letters, and Journals.* Edited by Ednah D. Cheney. Boston: Little, Brown, 1911.

Alexander, Andrew. "The Dunbar Letters: The Tragic Love Affair of One of America's Greatest Poets." *Washington Post Magazine,* June 28, 1981.

Ayers, Edward L. *The Promise of the New South: Life After Reconstruction.* New York: Oxford University Press, 1992.

Brown, Dorothy H., and Barbara C. Ewell. *Louisiana Women Writers: New Essays and Comprehensive Bibliography.* Baton Rouge: Louisiana University Press, 1992.

Carrigan, Jo Ann. "Yellow Fever: Scourge of the South." *Disease and Distinctiveness in the American South.* Edited by Todd L. Savitt and James Harvey Young. Knoxville: University of Tennessee Press, 1988.

Chopin, Kate. *The Awakening and Selected Stories of Kate Chopin.* New York: Signet Classic, 1976.

Cowan, Ruth Schwartz. *More Work for Mother: The Ironies of Household Technology from the Open Hearth to the Microwave.* London: Free Association Books, 1989.

Delamar, Gloria T. *Louisa May Alcott and "Little Women": Biography, Critique, Publications, Poems, Songs and Contemporary Relevance.* Jefferson, NC: McFarland & Company, 1990.

Dunbar-Nelson, Alice. *The Collected Works of Alice Dunbar-Nelson.* Vol. 1–3. Edited by Gloria T. Hull. The Schomburg Library of Nineteenth-Century Black Women Writers series. New York: Oxford University Press, 1988.

Elfenbein, Anna Shannon. *Women on the Color Line: Evolving Stereotypes and the Writings of George Washington Cable, Grace King, Kate Chopin.* Charlottesville: University of Virginia Press, 1991.

Evans, Sara M. *Born for Liberty: A History of Women in America.* New York: Free Press, 1989.

Forten Grimké, Charlotte. *The Journals of Charlotte Forten Grimké.* Edited by Brenda Stevenson. The Schomburg Library of Nineteenth-Century Black Women Writers series. New York: Oxford University Press, 1988.

Gilman, Charlotte Perkins. *The Diaries of Charlotte Perkins Gilman.* Vols. 1 and 2. Edited by Denise Knight. Charlottesville: University Press of Virginia, 1994.

———. *The Living of Charlotte Perkins Gilman.* 1935. Reprint. New York: Harper, 1975.

———. *The Yellow Wallpaper.* New York: Feminist Press, 1973.

Green, Harvey. *The Light of the Home: An Intimate View of the Lives of Women in Victorian America.* New York: Pantheon, 1983.

Harrison, William Henry. Introduction to *Transcendental Wild Oats and Excerpts from the Fruitlands Diary,* by Louisa May Alcott. Boston: Harvard Common Press, 1975.

Hull, Gloria T. *Color, Sex & Poetry: Three Women Writers of the Harlem Renaissance.* Bloomington: Indiana University Press, 1987.

———, ed. *Give Us This Day: The Diaries of Alice Dunbar-Nelson.* New York: Norton, 1984.

Jones, Jacqueline. *Soldiers of Light and Love: Northern Teachers and Georgia Blacks, 1865–1870.* Chapel Hill: University of North Carolina Press, 1980.

Kelley, Mary. *Private Woman, Public Stage: Literary Domesticity in Nineteenth-Century America.* New York: Oxford University Press, 1984.

Lane, Ann J. *To Herland and Beyond: The Life and Work of Charlotte Perkins Gilman.* New York: Pantheon, 1990.

Rankin, Daniel S. *Kate Chopin and Her Creole Stories.* Philadelphia: University of Pennsylvania Press, 1932.

Reilly, Wayne E., ed. *Sarah Jane Foster: Teacher of the Freedmen.* Charlottesville: University Press of Virginia, 1990.

Rose, Willie Lee. *Rehearsal for Reconstruction: The Port Royal Experiment.* New York: Vintage, 1967.

Saxton, Martha. *Louisa May: A Modern Biography of Louisa May Alcott.* Boston: Houghton Mifflin, 1977.

Seyersted, Per, and Emily Toth. *A Kate Chopin Miscellany.* Natchitoches, LA: Northwestern State University Press, 1979.

Shockley, Ann Allen. *Afro-American Women Writers 1746–1933: An Anthology and Critical Guide.* New York: Meridian, 1989.

Showalter, Elaine. *Sister's Choice: Tradition and Change in American Women's Writing.* Oxford: Clarendon, 1991.

Sterling, Dorothy, ed. *We Are Your Sisters: Black Women in the Nineteenth Century.* New York: Norton, 1984.

Stern, Madeleine. Introduction to *Behind a Mask: The Unknown Thrillers of Louisa May Alcott,* by Louisa May Alcott. New York: Morrow, 1975.

———. Introduction to *From Jo March's Attic: Stories of Intrigue and Suspense,* by Louisa May Alcott, Boston: Northeastern University Press, 1993.

———. Introduction to *Plots and Counterplots: More Unknown Thrillers of Louisa May Alcott,* by Louisa May Alcott. New York: Morrow, 1976.

Toth, Emily. *Kate Chopin,* New York: Morrow, 1990.

Turner, Lorenzo Dow. *Africanisms in the Gullah Dialect.* Chicago: University of Chicago Press, 1949.

Wells, Ida B. *Crusade for Justice: The Autobiography of Ida B. Wells.* Edited by Alfreda M. Duster. Chicago: University of Chicago Press, 1970.

Welter, Barbara. *Dimity Convictions: The American Woman in the Nineteenth Century.* Athens: Ohio University Press, 1976.

Woloch, Nancy. *Women and the American Experience.* New York: Knopf, 1994.

Books About Diaries

Culley, Margo. *A Day at a Time: The Diary Literature of American Women from 1764 to the Present.* New York: Feminist Press at the City University of New York, 1985.

Gannett, Cinthia. *Gender and the Journal: Diaries and Academic Discourse.* Albany: State University of New York Press, 1992.

Moffat, Mary Jane, and Charlotte Painter. *Revelations: Diaries of Women.* New York: Random, 1975.

Rainer, Tristine. *The New Diary: How to Use a Journal for Self-Guidance and Expanded Creativity.* Los Angeles: Jeremy P. Tarcher, 1978.

Stevens, Carla. *A Book of Your Own: Keeping a Diary or Journal.* New York: Clarion, 1993.

Index

DATE DUE

NOV	1 4 2002		
			Printed in USA